TANG CHINA

ECHOES OF THE ANCIENT WORLD

SERIES EDITOR
WERNER FORMAN

TANG CHINA

VISION AND SPLENDOUR OF A GOLDEN AGE

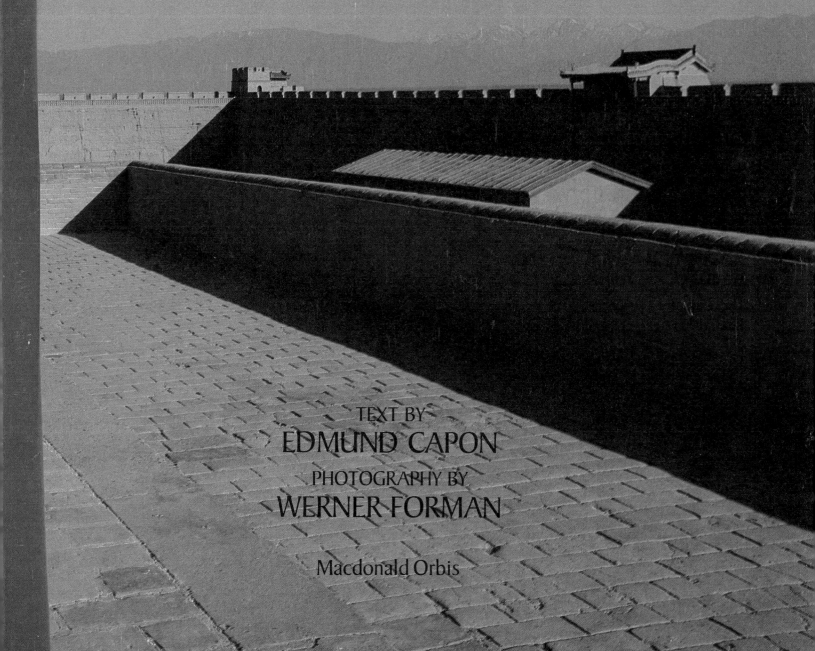

TEXT BY
EDMUND CAPON

PHOTOGRAPHY BY
WERNER FORMAN

Macdonald Orbis

A *Macdonald Orbis* BOOK
© Macdonald & Co (Publishers) Ltd 1989
Werner Forman's photographs © Werner Forman 1989

First published in Great Britain in 1989
by Macdonald & Co (Publishers) Ltd
London & Sydney

A member of Maxwell Pergamon Publishing Corporation plc

British Library Cataloguing in Publication Data

Capon, Edmund
    Tang China.—(Echoes of the ancient world).
    1. Chinese civilization, 618–906
    I. Title   II. Forman, Werner   III. Series
951'.01

ISBN 0–356–15674–5

Calligraphy by Dr Liu Weiping, University of Sydney

Photograph page 112 (left) © China Cultural Relics Publishing House

Filmset by August Filmsetting, Haydock, St Helens

Printed and bound in Portugal by Printer Portuguesa
Senior Editor:Catherine Rubinstein
Senior Art Editor: Philip Lord
Designer: William Mason

Macdonald & Co (Publishers) Ltd
Greater London House
Hampstead Road
London NW1 7QX

HALF TITLE PAGE *The Buddhist cave temples of Dunhuang were also the repository of treasures other than wall paintings and sculptures. Among the manuscripts, sutras, documents and silks preserved in the sealed caves were magnificent embroideries dating from the Tang dynasty such as this banner of the Buddha Sakyamuni preaching on Vulture Peak. The Buddha stands within an almond-shaped aureole behind which may be seen the rocky features of Mt Grdhrakuta or Vulture Peak. The senses of space and volume, which reflect the classic Tang feeling for naturalism found in the painted counterpart, are perfectly achieved here in the embroidered form.*

TITLE PAGE *The fortress of Jiayuguan marks the western end of the Great Wall in Gansu province. It was in these wilderness regions bordering the Central Asian deserts that the Tang empire encountered the nomadic peoples of Central and Western Asia who had travelled the Silk Road bringing foreign and exotic styles to the very heart of imperial China.*

CONTENTS

I

THE FOUNDING OF AN EMPIRE

The great Tang dynasty (AD 618–906) saw the transition of China from the 'ancient' phase of its history to the beginnings of its later or 'modern' history. In essence the dynasty established a cultural pattern that was to remain characteristic of China until the early decades of the twentieth century. A significant part of that pattern was the achievement of a national unity. Little wonder, then, that the Tang dynasty is generally acknowledged as a golden age in the history of China – the springboard from which later dynasties drew their inspiration, their style and, above all, their standards.

As soon as Li Yuan, who adopted the imperial title Emperor Gao Zu ('High Ancestor'), emerged victorious over the other clans to establish the Tang dynasty in AD 618, the historiographers and genealogists were set to create and confirm impeccable credentials for him – and thus indeed for the Tang dynasty itself. The scholars sought to establish a lineage into the deep past for the new Emperor, especially to the Royal House of China's first period of lasting imperial unity, the Han dynasty (206 BC–AD 220), that gleaming pearl of antiquity which was a perpetual reference point for the Tang Chinese.

It is perhaps the continuity and thus the stability of Chinese civilization and culture that has so fascinated the West, and Europe in particular, where history has been characterized by dramatic evolution through a cycle of renaissance and revolution. The reaching back into history on the part of Li Yuan of the Tang dynasty, and many other such founding emperors, in order to establish their credentials for assuming the 'Mandate of Heaven', is a critical aspect of the essential conservatism in Chinese society which contributed so substantially to the gradual and enduring evolutionary processes of Chinese civilization.

Indeed, it is with the historically symbolic Han dynasty that the story of the founding of the Tang begins. Apart from the short-lived Qin dynasty (221–06 BC) the Han was the only precedent for an enduring and unified Chinese empire. The preface to the founding of the Han Empire was also repeated at the founding of the Tang; for as the Han dynasty was preceded by a brief but immensely determined Qin dynasty, so the Sui dynasty (AD 581–618), some eight centuries later, established the foundations for the Tang. The cycle of events that brought the Han dynasty to power at the end of the third century BC created a situation of economic stability, peace, prosperity and territorial expansion, which was then followed by uncertainty in the early decades of the next millennium, leading to eventual

The Tang horse epitomizes the art of China. Glazed pottery models such as this were made solely for placement in the royal and aristocratic tombs of Tang China where, hidden for centuries, these beautiful works of art have ensured that the memory of the dynasty lives on. The power, nobility and gregarious artistry of the classic Tang horse is a poignant comment on the style and attitude of Tang China.

LEFT *Some 24km (15 miles) south-east of the Tang city of Jin Yang – present-day Taiyuan, capital of Shanxi province – lies the Jin Ci temple, founded in the fifth century. Here emperors built leisure palaces and gardens watered by the plentiful spring, and in 646 the second Tang emperor, Tai Zong, returned to write and inscribe a stele in recognition of the protection Prince Shu had granted his father. The cedar tree is said to date from the Tang dynasty. Li Yuan, founder of the Tang dynasty, launched his final assault on the fading Sui empire from nearby Jin Yang.*

BELOW *The precincts to the imperial tombs of the Tang are protected by monumental stone carvings of guardian figures and animals, the most important and familiar of which is the lion. The lion is not indigenous to China and was only introduced into the artistic and symbolic repertoire through Buddhism. Here the powerful snarling beast, an emblem of valour, strength and wisdom, guards the tomb of the mother of the infamous Empress Wu near the Tang imperial burial grounds at Qianling, north-west of Xian.*

intrigue, rebellion and collapse. This pattern was to be echoed by the Tang dynasty and, indeed, in the later history of China.

The Han dynasty followed the Bronze Age, a thirteen-century-long period during which the culture and achievement of China was characterized by bronze vessels, weapons and fittings displaying a technological and artistic attainment of the highest sophistication. The strength and unity of Bronze Age China was based on a concept of limited centralization of state and government embodied in the so-called 'city-state'. This system, reflecting the constraints of available communication facilities, focussed hereditary power on the capital but allowed for the emergence of small semi-autonomous principalities, notionally operating administratively within the overall framework of the centralized state. However, records indicate that as many as 150 to 200 of these semi-autonomous states which existed in the eighth century BC gained autonomy, leading to the eventual demise of the centralized state.

By the fifth century BC the situation in China had degenerated into what is aptly described as the Warring States period (475–221 BC). China, known as the 'Middle Kingdom' – the name being a literal translation of the characters for China – for three centuries experienced a political and social fragmentation that was the very antithesis of the centralized state. At this time the sole unifying feature of the diverse social, political and philosophical attitudes was the Chinese cultural umbrella, which has, of course, been the potent and pervasive force that has guided and defined a continuous civilization for over nine millennia.

ABOVE *A brightly coloured lead-glazed pottery rhyton cup reflects the confident style of the Tang in its adaptation of an imported shape with a handle in the form of a lotus; but it also shows the strength of tradition in the symbolic monster mask or taotie that was the most familiar decorative motif on ancient Chinese bronze vessels. This ferocious-looking mask with its part-dragon part-bovine features was traditionally regarded as a warning against greed, a legend that arose from an interpretation written as early as the third century BC which described the* taotie *as a monster with a head but no body that devoured men but before it could swallow them was itself attacked and eaten.*

ABOVE *The lead-glazed pottery vessels and tomb figures of the Tang dynasty express its very essence and flavour. The rich colours and opulent lotus-inspired form of this foliate dish capture the spirit, quality and vision of the art of the era.*

Those centuries of division were finally brought to an end by the Qin dynasty towards the end of the third century BC, under the inspired if dogmatic leadership of the dynasty's founder, Qin Shihuang. His achievement in establishing territorial unity and centralized government are acknowledged by historians in their recognition of Qin Shihuang as the founder of the Chinese Empire. The Qin dynasty's legacy to the Han was the foundation upon which it could consolidate and subsequently build a truly strong and enduring dynastic empire.

Through the achievements of Qin Shihuang the Han inherited the semblance of a unified empire, with those essential concepts of a centralized government and the rudiments of a structure through which that government and the court could function. Such a bureaucratic Utopia was not achieved immediately, for the founding emperor of the Han dynasty had first to acknowledge and pay off his relations and families loyal to him with princely and noble fiefdoms, thereby in fact increasing the risk of disunity. Gradually, however, these were brought under the overall jurisdiction of the central court and there then existed a style and structure of government which was to become the model for the Tang dynasty some eight centuries later.

But it was more the vision and style of the Han, and its total commitment to the expression of the Chinese ideal, from artistic style to the Confucian ethic, from filial piety to material dynamism, and from imperial unity to social bureaucracy, that so identified the Han dynasty as a classic model for the Tang.

The concept of the dynastic cycle has always been held as a valid and irrefutable aspect of historical change in China. Even the Han historians saw their dynasty, distinctive as it was, as part of that evolutionary repetitive process which had surfaced in the Bronze Age Shang and Zhou dynasties, and later historians saw the Tang dynasty as some kind of recycled Han dynasty. That there is some basis to the notion of repetitive dynastic momentum in the history of China, with great and cohesive dynasties of similar duration being followed by periods of disunity – often with non-Chinese intervention – and then a brief but dogmatic reunifying dynasty laying the foundations for another long period of stability, is undeniable. The Qin dynasty reunited China after the centuries of internecine conflict of the Warring States; the Han dynasty followed with nearly four centuries of relative peace, stability, economic and cultural growth; it, in turn, was succeeded by a long period of disunity that was brought to an end only by the resolute but brief Sui dynasty which laid the foundations for the succeeding Tang dynasty. The Tang dynasty too was followed by a period of division, known as the Five Dynasties, which was succeeded by the tenacious Song dynasty (AD 960–1279). Towards the end of the thirteenth century, China was divided once again by alien, on this occasion Mongol, rule under the Yuan dynasty (1279–1368), which was followed by the enduring, and pervasively Chinese, Ming dynasty (1368–1644). The non-Chinese, so-called 'barbarian' role in those periods of division that invariably followed one of the great imperial dynasties was a most significant one, particularly in coalescing the inherent forces of Chinese culture to evict the invaders and in bringing into the Middle Kingdom fresh styles and ideas which refreshed that very culture. A similar pattern in the historical evolutionary process that has tended to be the norm within the dynasty was development to a crescendo, generally early on in the dynasty, followed by gradual decline. In this respect, too, the history of the Han provides a precedent for the Tang.

In general, imperial lines in China tended to decline. The founding emperor was invariably a man of great strength, vision and ability, and it was often the case that his immediate successors were of equal merit. These emperors naturally benefited from the continuing drive of the originating momentum. In such cases a dynasty reached its peak of achievement, not at its birth, but generally some decades on. However, as time passed factions within the court emerged and eroded the unity and authority of government. They not only sowed the seeds of discontent at the centre of government but also made it possible for regional power bases to

ABOVE *According to ancient legend the first appearance of the phoenix in Chinese history was in the reign of the semi-mythical Yellow Emperor around 2600 BC. Supposed to appear only in times of peace and prosperity, the phoenix became in the Tang dynasty far more than just a mythological creature presiding over the southern quadrant of the heavens; it became virtually the symbol of the empress. This thin sheet-gold pair of phoenixes of the Tang dynasty would have ornamented the robes of an empress or imperial princess.*

develop. Weak and indeterminate leadership, which so often emerged in the imperial line after the passage of time, merely compounded the problems and led to eventual dissolution.

So it was that internal court problems, caused in particular by ambitious empresses, the unreasonable power of the eunuchs, and financial strains in the maintenance of such a vast empire, combined to bring to an end the first enduring Chinese imperial dynasty, the Han. Nevertheless, what that dynasty achieved was the creation of a model empire based on strong centralized government and a confident expansionism that was to provide China for 2000 years with a vital inspiration and a past which confirmed the supremacy of the Chinese ideal.

The demise of the Han dynasty in the early third century AD heralded a period of division in which non-Chinese people played a critical role. As the civil administration and the authority of the emperor evaporated, it was the powerful independent families, led by rich landowners, who adopted a military role that led the forces of change.

The period immediately after the fall of the Han dynasty is known as the Three Kingdoms. These states, those of Wei, Wu and Shu Han, were fragmented sections of the old empire that alluded to, rather than echoed, Han style and power. In a more determined effort, the eventual leader of the state of Wei (in north China), Sima Yan, overcame his neighbours and briefly reunited the Middle Kingdom under the name of the Jin dynasty. He grandly styled himself Jin Wudi, 'Martial Emperor of Jin', and clearly had visions of re-establishing the empire in the image of the Han. It was, however, a typical 'one-man' dynasty which fell apart shortly after Jin Wudi's death in 290 AD.

It is interesting to reflect on how, within the history of China, the brief Three Kingdoms period is viewed. For although it was clearly a time of dissension and failure characterized by incessant warfare, it is remembered by Chinese historians as an exciting and even romantic time. The great battles between the states and the leading clans gave rise to endless legends and numerous popular heroes. One of the principal figures, Guan Yu, a warrior of note and close friend of Liu Bei, founder of the Shu Han dynasty, even became canonized as Guan Di, the God of War. There is indeed an epic quality about this period of Chinese history. It is captured in the wonderfully named 'peach-garden oath' taken by Guan Yu, Liu Bei and another colleague shortly before the fall of the Han dynasty, which committed them to fight side by side and live and die together. However, it may be that this terrible time in Chinese history was immortalized as heroic out of a desire to redress the balance after the failure of the Han. The loss of the empire could perhaps be partially mitigated by the created heroes of the Three Kingdoms.

A most significant development, and one that was to profoundly affect the Tang dynasty, was the foothold gained by non-Chinese peoples in the agricultural lands of north China during the period that Han power was noticeably declining, in the first and second centuries AD. These were the very peoples who had been subjugated by the Han, semi-nomadic tribes of Mongol, Altaic or even Tibetan origin, yet generally Turkish speaking. These peoples had constantly been knocking on the door of China's northern borders. Their efforts had not been concerted and they had, therefore, been subjected to continual defeats at the hands of the Han. Gradually they were absorbed into north China where they settled down as semi-agricultural tribes principally in the modern provinces of Shanxi, Shaanxi and Henan. In the classic swing of the pendulum that the concept of *yin-yang* dualism evokes, it was the subjugation of these peoples that led to their rise to power.

From the beginning of the fourth century AD, and for the next three centuries, non-Chinese 'barbarians' were to play a constant and critical role in the formation and direction of Chinese life, particularly in the north in the Yellow River valley, the traditional heartland of Chinese power and civilization. This influx of non-Chinese tribes into the north forced large numbers of Han people to flee southwards, to mountainous regions of Sichuan and south of the Yangtze. The overall

effect of this substantial readjustment in China's population was the introduction of a mixed base to the population of north China, with all its cultural ramifications.

This essential division between a Chinese-controlled south China and a non-Chinese-controlled north China was to survive until the founding of the Sui dynasty in AD 581, although total reunification was not achieved until 589. What is perhaps unexpected is that in the historical perspective the initiative, in cultural terms particularly, seems to have remained in the north and did not, as one might have expected, move south with the more established Chinese population. It is possible that the traditional roots of Chinese civilization were so firmly established that the cultural momentum could not be dislodged.

Equally, it must be recognized that the rulers of north China at this time were culturally less dogmatic. The absence in their traditions of an unyielding social order with its attendant inflexibilities made the acceptance of new ideas and ideals possible. Traditional Chinese conservatism and the remorse felt at the failure of the Han dynasty must, on the other hand, have diluted the resolve of the Chinese population in the south.

But the 'barbaric' invasion must be seen in its proper perspective. In the historical and cultural evolution of China it influenced events far more than it actually directed them. These non-Chinese peoples were already present in Han dynasty China, and by the fourth century AD were truly settled into the established order. Even before their permanent presence in China, they had lived in the shadow of Chinese culture. Thus while they had neither the specific backgrounds nor the family associations and attendant concepts of responsibility that the Chinese had, the non-Chinese tribes of the border regions had certainly been conditioned by Chinese cultural patterns. When China weakened and the nomadic peoples were in the ascendancy they therefore found within the Great Wall not only kindred spirits but also familiar traditions well established in the more remote northern regions of China.

As history has shown, no invaders of China, from the Xiungnu Tartars of the third and fourth centuries to the Mongols of the late thirteenth and fourteenth centuries or the Manchus in the late seventeenth century, have ever imposed a new cultural direction upon China. In fact the reverse has always happened, with the invaders embracing the Chinese way of life.

The readjustment of the Chinese establishment during the period of division had the general effect of loosening the hold of traditional values and beliefs. Confucianism was no longer regarded as the sole source of philosophical and ideological aspiration as scholars sought fresh inspiration among Taoist, Buddhist and folklore traditions. And of course the presence of peoples less bound by traditional Chinese values assisted in the spread and development of such popular cults and beliefs.

The cumulative effect of such a fusion of new impulses and ideas was a thorough shake-up of Chinese society. But of even greater significance is the fact that, at the end of over three centuries of such social, cultural and administrative disturbance, the Chinese empire emerged under the Tang dynasty as strong and identifiable as it had ever been.

The fall of the Han dynasty in China is often compared to the fall of the Roman Empire. But whereas the latter never recovered from that reversal, the Chinese empire did recover, to flourish in the glory of even greater achievements. Nevertheless, a comparison of the two declines is a useful one, for it illustrates the tenacity and flexibility of those qualities that support the Chinese cultural and social systems. It is just those qualities that have maintained China as an identifiable and independent entity from the neolithic period of the sixth millennium BC to the present day. There are practical reasons too for its survival: its geographic isolation created by the natural barriers of deserts and steppelands to the north and west, mountains to the south and south-west and the ocean to the east; a distinctive writing system that was totally alien to other societies including the menacing

ABOVE *The expanding Tang empire encountered the nomadic tribes of Central Asia and the Mongolian steppelands. Here, at the eastern end of the Tian Shan mountains that run along the northern edge of the Taklamakan desert and form the border with the Soviet Union, live the horse-riding Kazak people. Today their distinctive portable tents or yurts, so well suited to their migratory life-style, have changed little from the times when the Tang armies extended the Chinese empire into the region.*

RIGHT *The maintenance and expansion of the Tang empire depended upon the mobility of its armies and they in turn depended upon the famed Ferghana horses, the steeds that have been immortalized in literature as the 'horses that sweated blood'. Pottery models made for tombs, such as this large, rare green-glazed example, have a sense of noble naturalism that echoes the esteem in which these proud and sturdy beasts were held in Tang China.*

Turkic tribes; a developed and structured social hierarchy that was difficult to penetrate; the maintenance of the Chinese style and ideal by the purely Chinese states in the south during the third to sixth centuries; and, finally, well-developed agricultural and technological capabilities which ensured self-reliance. Perhaps most important, these practical considerations were consolidated by the Chinese belief in the pre-eminence of their society and civilization. The Han dynasty really established the notion of the intrinsic superiority of the imperial court which was embodied in the fact that the Emperor of China ruled by divine right under the Mandate of Heaven. Even though the Han dynasty finally failed, those four centuries of achievement, unity and imperial splendour firmly established in the minds of the people an enduring expectation of China's ultimate and inevitable superiority. For the victorious invaders, the 'barbarians', to have failed totally

to impose their own traditions upon the conquered in the centuries that followed is extraordinary.

By the fourth century there were five main groups of semi-nomadic 'barbarian' tribes who had established a presence, generally in the form of a shortlived dynasty, in north China. They were of Turkic, Mongolian and Tibetan stock and it was the Turkic peoples who were to have the most significant influence upon events in China and indeed to contribute the most important achievements. In 386 a Turkic tribe known as the Toba established the Northern Wei dynasty in central north China. By 439 the Northern Wei had defeated the last of its rivals in the north and thus reunited China north of the Yangtze, albeit under a foreign banner. The subsequent transformation of the Toba ruling house from nomadic Turkic invader to a seemly occupant of the Chinese imperial court was completed by the end of the fifth century when the Northern Wei relocated their capital at Loyang in the centre of the Yellow River basin and the court consciously adopted Chinese styles, customs, habits and values.

As a result of the Northern Wei court's total commitment to the Chinese style and ethic, some tribal elders were left by the wayside. Rebellions broke out in peripheral and border communities which felt that they had been neglected. By the middle of the sixth century, Northern Wei unity had given way to a resurgence of 'barbaric' power with the division of that empire into the Eastern Wei, occupying the north-east, and the Western Wei in the western regions. These two brief dynasties were followed by the Northern Qi and Northern Zhou respectively, with the latter rapidly emerging as the more powerful of the two.

Although these dynasties in the second half of the sixth century did reflect a resurgence of non-Chinese power it would be inaccurate to suggest that this was synonymous with a decline in Chinese presence, or indeed of Chinese influence. For by this time all the 'barbarian' ruling houses had become substantially inter-married with established Chinese families, including no less a family than that of the founder of the Tang dynasty.

The founder of the Sui dynasty, Yang Jian, while claiming pure Chinese descent, was related to the ruling house of the Northern Zhou and thus almost certainly had some Turkic blood. Yang, who adopted the imperial title Wen Di, 'Cultural Emperor', achieved a role in the history of China comparable to that of Qin Shihuang some eight centuries before. Like Qin, Wen Di unified the empire, centralized government, reconstructed the defensive Great Wall, built huge and impressive palaces and fortresses, and reconstituted the communications system. In particular Wen Di instituted the construction and development of China's invaluable canal system.

However, also like the Qin, the Sui was shortlived and barely survived the death of its founder in 604. Both dynasties were the complete achievement of their founders, and without the character, determination and vision of those men the unifying forces were lost. Both emperors were succeeded by sons whose claim to the Mandate of Heaven was not matched by their ability. Indeed Wen Di's son Yang Di, or 'Emblazoned Emperor', is generally regarded in the histories of China as a villain. In this respect, particularly, the Tang dynasty differs, for it is perhaps in the succession of great emperors that its real achievements lie.

Wen Di founded the Sui capital at Changan (present-day Xian), thereby echoing the glories of the past, for that city had served as the capital of Han, as it did for the succeeding Tang. His first concern was to consolidate the empire and secure its borders. The early years of the Sui saw Chinese control reasserted over North Vietnam and large areas of Central Asia, regions whose peoples were a constant threat to the Chinese empire. Wen Di's successor, Yang Di, sought to emulate the expansive military campaigns into the still unsubdued territories of Korea and Manchuria. It was largely due to the failure of these extravagant sorties that uprisings and rebellions against him developed, which were to lead to the eventual downfall of the dynasty.

ABOVE *A pottery figure glazed in blue, green and amber of a dignified lady holding a bird echoes the flavour of Tang court life. The theme of ladies holding birds is repeated in much tomb decoration, including wall paintings and the incised designs on the stone sarcophagus of, for example, Princess Yong Tai, who was buried at the imperial tomb complex at Qianling in 706.*

RIGHT *As the Tang empire extended its control over the northern and north-western borderlands, so the vanquished peoples were brought into service. The imperial courts and stables were largely manned by such people, often regarded by the Chinese with both fascination and aversion, hence the caricature-like face of this pottery model of a groom.*

LEFT *Although work on the building of the Great Wall began in the late Bronze Age, some ten centuries before the establishment of the Tang dynasty, it continued to serve its defensive role up to the Ming and even the Qing dynasties. During the Tang the extent of the empire was such that the Great Wall was almost entirely within Chinese territory and its defensive function was lost, but it remained useful for communications.*

As Qin Shihuang and the founder of the Han dynasty, Gao Zi, had done before, and Gao Zu of the Tang and others were to do later, Wen Di sought to further consolidate his empire through a substantial programme of construction and public works. In addition to the palaces and canals, roads and state granaries were all part of that achievement, intended not only to provide effective and practical resources but also to reflect the power and strength of the new court in buildings that might well outlive the dynasty and thereby provide later generations with an image of grandeur. Founding emperors, it seemed, were inspired by Qin Shihuang's statement that his dynasty would 'live for a thousand years' and great palaces and constructions would serve as testimony to dynastic longevity.

The fading years of the Sui dynasty saw Yang Di desperately clinging to his rapidly fragmenting empire. The final onslaught was brought about by China's traditional northern foes, the Turks. With Yang Di's armies committed to ill-fated Korean campaigns, the Turks took advantage of their absence from the north-western defences, and in the walled town of Yanwen, in present-day Shanxi province, the Emperor of China was trapped for a month by the marauding Turkish forces.

Accounts vary as to how the Emperor was released, but one of them attributes the achievement to none other than the fifteen-year-old Li Shimin, son of Li Yuan, who was destined to become the second emperor of the Tang dynasty. Li Shimin is said to have advised the general in command of the relieving force that the way to dispel the Turks was to spread his forces over a large area and, brandishing massed pennants by day and beating drums by night, to hoodwink the Turks into believing that the Chinese forces were very much larger than they really were. According to this account the ploy was successful and the Turks retreated. Even so, for the Emperor of China to be ensnared for a month by 'barbarian' Turks was a bitter blow to the prestige of the custodian of the Mandate of Heaven and another severe reversal in the fortunes of the Sui dynasty.

From this time on, Emperor Yang was on the defensive. His authority and credibility severely diminished, he returned to his 'eastern' capital at Loyang, abandoning all his grand construction schemes and military campaigns in order to devote his energies to mere survival. Internal disorders in the empire multiplied and the Emperor found little support even within the court.

One of the most evocative statements of how people felt about the Sui is recorded in a brief ballad which was then very popular and was to become even

RIGHT *The tombs of members of the royal family and other dignitaries of the Tang dynasty were always richly furnished with works of art, as remembrances of the deceased's life on earth. In numerical terms the most significant were the pottery tomb figures, models such as these of a trumpeter and a drummer from a retinue of military figures. Such was the popularity of the tradition in the Tang dynasty that an imperial edict was issued regulating the number and type of such figures that were to be placed in tombs according to rank.*

17

more popular at the time of the uprising in 617 of Li Yuan, the Duke of Tang. The ballad reads innocuously enough:

Peach plum Li
Be reserved in speech.
As a yellow heron you fly around the hill
And turn about within the flower garden.[1]

Closer analysis reveals that the lines are a positive incitement to rebellion. It identifies a certain Li Mi, who was later to become a leading figure in the anti-Sui uprisings. The yellow heron as a high-flying bird symbolizes ambition, and the hill and the garden combined refer to the Sui Empire. The ballad was, therefore, an encouragement to Li Mi, and indeed perhaps to any other popular leader with the name Li, to sustain the rebels' ambition and overthrow the Sui. Naturally the ballad and its connotations were brought to the attention of the Emperor, whose mistrust of any leading figure with the name Li immediately increased.

In 616 Emperor Yang withdrew to his southern capital and ceased to play any significant role in the affairs of state. The critical northern lands were left open to conflict among various rebel and bandit groups, with the old Sui commanders endeavouring to maintain order. Once again the determining events in Chinese history took place in the north.

Gradually power in north China coalesced into the hands of three rebel groups: those led by Dou Jiande in the north-east; those in the Loyang region, led by Li Mi – of ballad fame – who in 616–17 offered the greatest threat to the dynasty through his base near the Sui capital; and those led by Xie Ju in the north-west.

At this time, Li Yuan, Duke of Tang, was still a loyal, if distant, subject of the Sui Emperor, commanding imperial forces against rebel units in northern Shanxi province. Having defeated both the rebels in the south of the province and the Turks in the north, by 617 Li Yuan had emerged as the most powerful figure in Shanxi and was appointed Garrison Commander of the city of Taiyuan. Li Yuan was still recognized as a member of the royal Sui house, by marriage, with a distinguished record of military service. In many respects, therefore, he represented a semblance of traditional power, authority and stability in an increasingly unstable world. He had the surname Li, too, which, thanks in part to the famous ballad, was by then synonymous with prophetic power.

While in theory still an arm of the Sui dynasty, Li Yuan was virtually out of reach of reasonable contact with the court, which was by then located in the south. The initiatives for any action in such circumstances lay with the local commander. With both rebel groups and Turkic tribes continually harassing, action was required and there could be no delay to await instructions from the court. Aided and encouraged by his second son Li Shimin, Li Yuan took the initiative and in doing so formally abandoned his commitment to the Sui. Leaving his first son in charge at Taiyuan, Li Yuan marched on Changan, the original Sui capital which was even then still widely regarded as the traditional seat of imperial power in China. Having taken Changan, one of Li Yuan's first actions was to institute a new set of laws, as the *Tang Shu (The Book of Tang)* records:

He ordered the Secretary in charge of the Official Tallies, Song Gongbi, to collect the official documents and to reduce the laws to twelve articles. Murderers, thieves and robbers, deserters from the army, and those who rebelled were to be put to death.[2]

In issuing such an edict Li Yuan had adopted an imperial prerogative and he did so in the style and manner adopted by the founder of the Han dynasty in 206 BC. The historical precedent and the glowing image of the Han dynasty was already becoming apparent even at so early a stage in the evolution of the Tang dynasty.

The sheer presence of the officials and palace ladies of the Tang court that so impressed any visitor to Changan are captured in this blue-glazed pottery figure of a court lady. Her imposing demeanour and graceful proportions reflect the Tang style, but so too does the attention to detail in the sweeping robes and sleeves, the upturned shoes and facial features.

Meanwhile armies in the name of the Duke of Tang were progressing eastwards, southwards and westwards.

With this concentration of history-making activity in the north, south China had become a mere observer. Nevertheless south China was where the Sui Emperor still survived and China was still, nominally, under Sui rule. This changed dramatically on 11 April 618, when the Emperor was murdered by disenchanted colleagues and associates at the court. With the death of Yang Di all semblance of a unified Sui empire evaporated. There followed a brief hiatus while various claimants to the throne were supported, or even set up.

The Li family was by no means the only great and powerful clan in China at the turn of the seventh century. In the north there were many such clans, generally with a significant admixture of non-Chinese Turkic blood, with distinguished military backgrounds, in many respects equally powerful claimants to the Mandate of Heaven. In the south there were other great clans, generally with less distinguished military credentials, but of purer Chinese stock, who could trace their descent back to the Han ruling house some six or seven centuries earlier. Any one of a number of such clans could lay justifiable claim, substantiated through distinguished lineage, to the throne. Nonetheless the Li clan was in the vanguard, and Li Yuan and his court were of course well aware of their colleague families and clans that might threaten the new order. But the momentum behind Li Yuan and the dissolution of the Sui was by then irreversible. On 18 June 618 Li Yuan formally ascended the throne, accepted the Mandate of Heaven and established the glorious Tang dynasty that was to rule China for the next three centuries.

While it was Li Yuan and the Li family that had emerged victorious to found the Tang dynasty, and while that victory was achieved only with the support of other great clans, not only from the Shaanxi base of the Li family but also from those clans centred in northern Shanxi, the power of other traditional family groupings could not be overlooked. Families established for centuries within a region built up a network of influence and power through structures and chains of command that simply became recognized as 'the system'. Any attempt by the new emperor to dislodge these families and clans from their traditional homelands would have resulted in immediate rebellion. These powerful groups had to be gently and gradually brought into the system that was the centralized Tang government and, of course, through being absorbed, to become part of that structure. In the establishment of the Tang dynasty these aristocratic clans remained a most influential force. Any one of these powerful clan groups could have regarded itself as having a legitimate claim to the Mandate of Heaven so it was essential that the new Tang government should maintain a balance of power between them.

In many respects the natural authority and inheritance of power that devolved upon such clans was a factor contributing to that supreme confidence which characterized the Tang dynasty. There existed a perpetual air of expectancy fuelled by the gregarious attitude of the court. The composition of the ruling class was the clue to this founding strength, as the eighth-to-ninth-century scholar Su Mian records in his administrative encyclopedia, the *Hui Yao (Essential Regulations)*:

> . . . all the chief ministers who assisted in the founding of the present dynasty came from the great aristocratic clans. Ever since the three dynasties of antiquity there has never been any dynasty so distinguished by its aristocratic origins as the ruling house of the Tang.[3]

This may seem to be at odds with the notion of incipient conflict between the leading aristocratic clans; it is nonetheless a fact that later historians recalled the Tang as a period of classic stability, and that that condition was largely due to the pervasive strength of the great clans. What the founding emperors of the Tang quickly achieved was an administration that effectively involved the great clans, thereby blunting their possible reasons for seeking individual supremacy.

One of the monumental stone carvings of an official wearing a Confucian-style hat that line the 'spirit road' leading to the tomb of Emperor Gao Zong and Empress Wu at Qianling. These imposing larger-than-life-size carvings, representing the custodians of the Tang hierarchy and bureaucracy, are among the few examples of monumental figurative sculpture that have survived in China till today.

2
THE MANDATE OF HEAVEN

The Emperor of China was regarded as sovereign not merely of the Middle Kingdom but of 'all under heaven', that is, the Earth. He was the Son of Heaven, and Heaven had but one sun, one moon, and thus only one son. The emperor was far more than wise counsellor, diligent administrator and inspired military tactician: he was a human manifestation of the powers that shaped the universe, serving as emperor with the consent, or mandate, of Heaven.

Should the emperor fail to meet the required standards, the mandate to rule would be forfeited and his reign would end. Founding emperors, such as Gao Zu, could perhaps lay stronger claim to the mandate than others, because circumstances had determined that it should be passed from one ruling family to another, and that clearly reflected an almost conscious decision on the part of Heaven. In this practically deified role, the emperor was regarded as the manifestation of power and of virtue. As general arbiter and inspiration, it was thought, especially by that architect of the Chinese ethic, Confucius, that the emperor should not become involved in administration; participation in the mundane affairs of day-to-day life was considered incompatible with his role as mediator between Heaven and Earth.

The notion that the Emperor of China was the Son of Heaven was substantiated by references, particularly in late Zhou times (sixth to fifth centuries BC), to the role and style of the great so-called 'sage kings' of remote antiquity. Those shadowy figures were the culture-heroes who, as arms of the universe itself, actually shaped our planet: the creator Pan Gu, the twelve Celestial Sovereigns, the eleven Terrestrial Sovereigns and the nine Human Sovereigns represented Heaven, Earth and Man. They were followed by a series of emperors who provided the basic elements of civilization: the Yellow Emperor, who invented the compass, the calendar, boats, carts and other useful things; Shen Nong, who invented agriculture; the model emperors of great longevity, Yao and Shun, who created new ideas on the succession; Fuxi, who invented writing; and Yu, who carved the waterways.

Although later emperors were seen as more human and less immortal, something of this spiritual aura survived to surround them. Certainly, emperors of China were thought to have some kind of 'special relationship' with the powers of the Universe and Heaven. At times the emperor might submit to the temptation of becoming involved in the practicalities of government, but when he did it was taken as a sign of weakness. In accordance with this view was the precept that the emperor would select for his administration only men of wisdom, virtue and

The great stele on the summit of Taishan in Shandong province, where emperors performed the important feng *and* shan *sacrifices to the Heavens and Earth respectively. Known as the 'Stele Engraved on the Rock', this inscription was composed by the Tang Emperor Xuan Zong when he performed the feng sacrifice in 726, and later engraved on the rock, which measures 8.8 × 4.8 m (29 × 16 ft).*

The reverse side of a bronze mirror with a design of mythological subjects. The reflecting side is slightly convex and highly polished. The reverse side traditionally became a vehicle for the expression of mythological notions: here the outer rim illustrates the animals of the four quarters – the tortoise of the north, the dragon of the east, the bird of the south and the tiger of the west; the central area illustrates the hare pounding the mortar under the cassia tree, which stems from the toad representing Chang E who stole the Elixir of Immortality, fled to the moon and changed into a toad – these are traditional symbols of the moon. On the left is Xi Wangmu, the Queen Mother of the West, and below are the Mountains of the Immortals.

learning, truly within the Confucian ideal. In this excerpt from the *Huai Nan Zi*, a collection of essays and writings compiled by scholars in the second century BC at the court of the Han dynasty prince Huai Nan, the views expressed represent a synthesis of Confucian and Taoist ideals in summarizing the role of an emperor:

> The craft of the ruler consists in disposing of affairs without action and issuing orders without speaking. The ruler remains still and pure without moving, impartial without wavering. Compliantly, he delegates affairs to his subordinates and without troubling himself exacts success from them. Thus, though he has plans in his mind, he allows his counsellors to proclaim them; though his mouth can speak, he allows his administrators to talk for him; though his feet can walk, he lets his ministers lead; and though he has ears to hear, he permits the officials to remonstrate with him. Thus among his policies are none that fail and among his plans none that go awry . . . .[1]

This echoes Confucius's own views as recorded in the *Analects*:

> The Master [Confucius] said: 'He who exercises government by means of his virtue may be compared to the north polar star, which keeps its place and all the stars turn towards it.
>
> 'If the people be led by laws, and uniformity sought to be given them by punishments, they will try to avoid the punishment, but have no sense of shame.
>
> 'If they be led by virtue, and uniformity sought to be given them by the ruler of propriety, they will have the sense of shame, and moreover, will become good.'[2]

The Confucian disciple Mencius (fourth century BC) reasserted this point, again one that was firmly entrenched in the ethic of the Han and Tang rulers:

Mencius said: 'The people are the most important element in a nation; the spirits of the land and grain are the next; the sovereign is the lightest. Therefore to gain the peasantry is the way to become emperor; to gain the emperor is the way to become a prince of a State; to gain the prince of a State is the way to become a great officer. When a prince endangers the altars of the spirits of the land and grain, he is changed, and another appointed in his place. When the sacrificial victims have been perfect, the millet in its vessels all pure, and the sacrifices offered at their proper seasons, if yet there ensue drought, or the waters over-flow, the spirits of the land and grain are changed, and others are appointed in their place.'[3]

A later, third-century BC, Confucian philosopher proposed a more dogmatic interpretation, one that was to become the basis of the Legalist Doctrine. This doctrine, as its name suggests, maintained that good government could be exercised only through strict adherence to the law, and also reaffirmed the principle that if the emperor did not meet the expectations of the people, his mandate would be removed:

The ruler is the boat and the common people are the water. It is the water that bears the boat up and the water that capsizes it.[4]

The Mandate of Heaven doctrine was originally formulated by later Zhou rulers who claimed that Heaven had been displeased with the preceding Shang kings. The later Shang kings were deemed to have acted self-interestedly, ignoring the well-being of the people. Thus the mandate was removed. The notion of the mandate is not so much a positive guide for selecting an emperor as a measure for assessing performance. Dissatisfaction with the imperial order would be reflected in rebellion, uprisings and disorder among the people, while Heaven might express its views through such natural phenomena as earthquakes, droughts and floods.

The point of contact between the people and the emperor was the administration. The selection and appointment of officials was perhaps the emperor's greatest concern, for it was they who were to interpret and express the imperial quality and virtue as harmonious government as well as transmit the people's will back to the emperor.

The masses of officials, or mandarins, at the court of Gao Zu were not the only protagonists whom the Emperor had to take into account. He needed to consider other members of the imperial family, families of other powerful and influential aristocratic groups, and all those who had assisted him to victory. Ideals ran high in the founding years of a dynasty, but the exercise of these ideals had to be carefully tempered by considering the wishes of those who, in the tentative years, could so easily undermine the young dynasty.

Gao Zu inherited from the preceding Sui dynasty the form of a bureaucracy which served as a foundation for the new Tang government. Furthermore, he had to rely on a still relatively small number of confirmed allies who had some experience of administration. Indeed, no fewer than eight of his twelve chief ministers were related by marriage to the Sui and Tang imperial families. In the early days of the Tang dynasty a very few *dramatis personae* emerged as critical figures in a relatively small and elite hierarchy of administrators and advisers that determined the lives of tens of millions of subjects, even though only three million households were registered at the time (against nine million during the preceding Sui dynasty).

The administrators upon whom Gao Zu relied most were men such as Pei Ji, a close friend of his whose daughter married the Emperor's sixth son. Pei Ji, as a Sui official, had assisted the then Li Yuan in providing the Tang army with supplies and provisions. With the Tang victory he was amply rewarded with an appointment as head of the Department of State Affairs. The benefits to be reaped by transferring allegiance to the Tang is typified by the case of Xiao Yu, who had once even occupied the throne of the minor Liang dynasty in the south before serving the Sui. With the Tang victory this dextrous administrator transferred his loyalties to the Tang and served the dynasty's first two emperors as President of the Secretariat and Vice-President of the Department of State Affairs. His one failing was, it seems, an ungovernable temper which the second Tang emperor, Tai Zong, noted when Xiao Yu died at the age of seventy-four. Upon his death Xiao Yu was canonized as 'reverential', but the Emperor subsequently declared such a title to be unsuited to his temperament and changed the memorial to 'pure but narrow'.

It was through such officials that the founding Tang Emperor established an administration with at least some experience in government. Another point of significance that emerges from any review of Gao Zu's chief ministers is that he had not only to reward those who had assisted and supported him but also those with regional or factional power bases that could still unsettle the fragile Tang court. Whether by chance or design, and the latter would certainly seem to be the more likely and characteristic, Gao Zu selected his chief ministers well and achieved a balance of regional representation.

The administrative structure that the Tang adopted was, in essence, inherited from the Sui dynasty and, with minor amendments and refinements, survived in that form throughout the dynasty. There were three main components of central government: the Secretariat, the Chancellery and the Department of State Affairs. The Secretariat was notionally the most important organ of government in that it originated government policies and imperial edicts and drafted all promulgations. The Chancellery was the stronghold of bureaucratic power in its capacity as a reviewing body for all the Secretariat's pronouncements. In the practice of the administration of the Empire, the Department of State Affairs was the most important, with responsibility for the day-to-day functioning of the administration and the execution of orders. The Department exercised its authority through six ministries, or boards: for the civil service, finance, rites, the military, justice and public works. At the very heart of central government there was one more body of some significance, the Censorate. This was a unique and, in appearance at least, extraordinarily democratic organ of government whose task it was to monitor the progress of the highest administrative officers. The Censorate had a general responsibility for overseeing the work of the three principal bodies and investigating any cases of misgovernment, injustice or crime. To a lesser degree the officials of the Censorate were also charged with the traditional scholars' function of pointing out to the emperor any weaknesses or failures on his part.

The administration of the court itself was largely in the hands of the so-called 'Nine Courts', with separate boards for such affairs as sacrifices and ceremonies, the imperial household and judicial review.

All the principal officials serving within this complex but orderly structure had prescribed titles, a set number of subordinates and clearly defined responsibilities. Every position within the hierarchy was accorded a rank and officials at the appropriate level were appointed to fulfil that role.

Effective administration of a far-flung empire could by no means be entirely carried out from the capital city of Changan. Local government was a vital part of the Tang hierarchy and, like its central counterpart, the system was in principal inherited from the preceding Sui. Beneath the central government the chief administrative unit was the prefecture (*zhou*) and then the sub-prefecture (*xian*), which would now be referred to as counties or districts. These two administrative units were governed by prefects (*cishi*) and county magistrates (*xianling*) respectively. The overall management of the regions was further streamlined by the second emperor, Tai Zong, who instituted, above the prefectures and districts, ten *dao*, meaning 'routes' or 'circuits', which were administrative regions based on convenient routes for imperial officials, messengers or inspectors to follow in the exercise of their duties.

One inevitable effect of the centralization of government was that the capital,

The greatest architectural statement of the Chinese imperial structure and bureaucracy is the Forbidden City in Beijing. Built in the early fifteenth century, long after the Tang dynasty, the Palace still reflects the Tang ideal in its architectural style and the sense of authority in its layout.

Changan, became the main focus of attention and source of inspiration. In spite of being a rural economy with the vast majority of the population employed on the land, the China of the Tang dynasty was characterized by its urban and metropolitan achievements. There was, therefore, a tendency for the empire to split into metropolitan camps (principally the capital city of Changan) and rural camps. Ambitious officials looked upon a position in the regions as a severe setback, however important the responsibilities involved.

In addition to this extensive civil administration the Tang court also maintained a sizeable and widespread military establishment. Two standing armies were maintained at the capital. Throughout the empire forty-three regional military commands were established and these had authority over the local civil administration. Beneath the commands were local units. As many as 633 were established within the reign of the first emperor, each with up to 1200 soldiers. The military system differed slightly from its civil counterpart, in that serving soldiers were constantly rotated, doing service at the capital on a relatively regular basis. In this way, a sense of identity with the capital was maintained and local military units were prevented from gathering unreasonable strength and power in isolation. The military establishment of Tang China remained basically the same throughout the dynasty with slight amendments and refinements; one such was the Emperor Tai Zong's reorganization of the local units, which from then on were colourfully known as the *zhechong-fu* or the 'intrepid militia'.

This sophisticated structure of the civil and military administrations was established in the interests of securing and maintaining the empire. The longevity and grandeur of the dynasty was the most vital concern for any emperor, since it reflected a successful meeting of the demands of the Mandate of Heaven. Gao Zu's second son, Li Shimin, who ascended the throne in 626 as the Emperor Tai Zong, was determined to secure the dynasty for which he had fought so hard. One way of ensuring its longevity that was considered was the re-introduction of a form of feudalism by which princes and the highest ministers of state would be granted fiefs over which they and their heirs would rule. But these plans for a limited feudalism were finally abandoned and the system that had ceased to exist in China in the third century BC, but which survived in Europe until the end of the fifteenth century, was never again seriously considered as a form of policy in China.

It is possible that Tai Zong saw the re-introduction of a feudal system as one way of blunting the still considerable authority and influence, especially at local level, of the four great clans. After more than two decades of Tang rule, the power of these old-established families had still not been seriously eroded, so they did constitute a threat to the imperial household. In 632, the Emperor ordered a survey of the genealogies of the empire's most important clans. To his fury, the report classified the lineage of one of his minister's families first, with the imperial Li lineage being placed a lowly third. Not surprisingly, he rejected the report and in so doing suggested precisely how it should be revised. The second edition diplomatically placed the imperial line first, along with those families of the very highest-ranking ministers. Thus Tai Zong effectively re-wrote the social hierarchy of China, removing from the highest status the traditional clans and placing that mantle on the highest levels of the administration. This was to have a profound effect in the long term because as the administration gradually fell into the hands of professional civil servants admitted through the examination system, so it opened up the higher echelons of the social hierarchy to people from sectors of the community who would otherwise have had no access to them.

This admission of leaders whose credentials lay in their abilities rather than in the circumstances of their birth is highlighted by the life of one of the greatest and most powerful counsellors and ministers of the Tang dynasty. Wei Zheng was born in the founding year of the Sui dynasty, and not into obscurity, for his family had provided a long line of officials and historians to the Northern Wei, Northern Qi and Sui dynasties. However, he was orphaned at an early age and certainly had no assured future. His devoutly Confucian education was of little value in his early life, when the conflicts that witnessed the fall of the Sui dynasty were in progress. After serving anti-Sui rebels, Wei arrived in the Tang capital and apparently within a month secured himself a position, relatively lowly, as assistant in the Department of the Imperial Library, a post classified as one of the fifth rank. During Gao Zu's reign, Wei made solid if unspectacular progress. Those early years of the dynasty were characterized by the effects of lingering conflict and some uncertainty, which led the court to emphasize its military presence. Wei Zheng was a true Confucian scholar, and found himself somewhat ill at ease as a military-political official. By 626, when Tai Zong ascended the throne, the empire was at peace and the court reflected that condition in a strong civil, rather than military, bureaucracy. These changed circumstances allowed Wei Zheng to flourish as a classic Confucian scholar-official, and indeed his achievement typifies the quality of Tang China under Tai Zong's reign.

A 'talented generalist', in the true mould of the ideal Confucianist, Wei served the Emperor in a number of varied roles – as historian, bibliographer, ritualist, poet, tutor and adviser, in addition to his sundry official duties as a member of the Council of State, where he had jurisdiction over the Boards of War, Justice and

A painted stucco model of a soldier that was discovered in a shrine at Ming-oi, a remote outpost on the northern Silk Road midway between Turfan and Kizil where units of Tai Zong's 'intrepid militia' protected China's precious trade route. It is thought that the Tang soldier was relatively well equipped, and this model shows the typical military accoutrements of leather helmet, scale-armour which may have been either lacquered leather or iron, spear and circular shield.

Public Works. Other promotions followed, and finally he was appointed president of the commission for drawing up the *History of the Sui Dynasty*. This might seem the ultimate sinecure to us, but the fact that such a task should be entrusted to one of the Emperor's closest and most trusted advisers indicates a set of values very different from ours. Setting the historical record straight, and thus establishing the rights of that particular regime to the Mandate of Heaven, was thought to be of the utmost importance. Upon the death of Wei Zheng, the Emperor said:

> You may use copper as a mirror for the person; you may use the past as a mirror for politics; and you may use man as a mirror to guide the judgment in ordinary affairs. These three mirrors I have always carefully cherished; but now that Wei Zheng is gone, I have lost one of them.[5]

So imbued with the Confucian virtues was Wei Zheng that he frequently remonstrated with the Emperor when he felt the ruler was erring on the side of self-indulgence. When he learned of the Emperor's plans, in 637, to construct a new and lavish palace at Loyang, the so-called 'eastern capital' of the Tang, Wei's reaction was typical. He submitted a memorial advising the Emperor to return to a more frugal life:

> Now you occupy all the palaces and pavilions of the Empire. You have totally appropriated all the riches and treasures of the Sui dynasty. You have all Yang Di's [the Sui Emperor] concubines and women serving you. People in the Four Seas and the Nine Continents have all become your slaves and servants. If you are able to hold up to a mirror the reasons why he [Sui Yang Di] was destroyed and reflect upon the reasons why we gained the Empire, keep alert every day and never ease up even when you are at rest. Burn the precious garments of the Lutai [the 'deer park' where the last, and thus failed, king of the Shang dynasty of the eleventh century BC kept his treasure] and destroy the spacious halls of the Afang palace [the huge palace complex built by Qin Shihuang at Xianyang in the third century BC]. Fear the danger and destruction that comes from living in lofty palaces and give thought to living peacefully in humble surroundings, then you will undergo a divine transformation and rule by non-activity. This is the highest virtue.[6]

As a champion of the Confucian bureaucracy, Wei Zheng would certainly have supported the machinery that allowed for the real development of that bureaucracy in the Tai Zong reign, and which continued to flourish and grow throughout the Tang dynasty. This was, of course, the civil service examination system. Limited entry to the schools that provided the official examinations prevented widespread access to the rarified world of court politics, and in social terms China's administration remained in the hands of the aristocracy. What the examination system did achieve, however, was wider access on the basis of education rather than hereditary privilege. The effects of this system gathered slow but effective force in the seventh century and then progressed rapidly under the administration of the Empress Wu (reigned 690–705). As this extraordinary woman (of whom more later) was not a direct descendant of the Li family, she was without substantial aristocratic backing, and thus she sought to establish her court with successful candidates, who had no allegiance to any aristocratic line, through the examination system. After the reign of the Empress Wu, Tang court politics became polarized between the 'old aristocrats', back in the driving seat after Empress Wu had been deposed, and the 'new bureaucrats' who by then had their feet firmly in the door of the court. It was the latter group, the professionals, who finally emerged as the new elite of the late Tang dynasty.

The composition of the bureaucracy was based on three levels of official service. Firstly, the true mandarins or officials, called the *guan*; secondly, those known as the

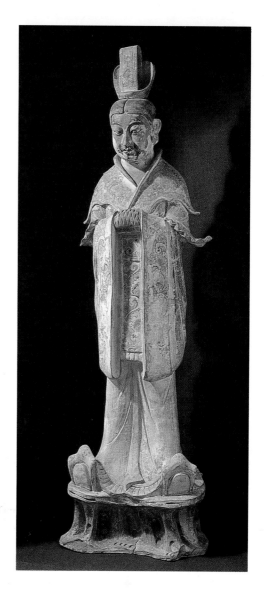

An unglazed pottery model of a Tang courtier, with features painted with unfired pigments and some gilding. As such tomb figures were facsimiles of reality, great attention was paid to the detail in order to achieve a lifelike finish; in this example the facial features, costume details and textile patterns are all rendered with precision and remarkably well preserved.

liuwai-guan which, literally translated, means 'officials outside the current', that is, officials who were not privy to decisions or the processes of decision-making but merely carried out orders in an essentially clerical capacity; and thirdly, many thousands of minor employees who served the state in menial capacities from gardeners to servants. In the early eighth century there were approximately 19,000 *guan* in office (2500 in central government at the capital, and the remainder in the regions) and approximately 56,000 *liuwai-guan*. This sizeable administration controlled an empire with a registered population of between forty and fifty million, which in reality was probably closer to seventy million. By today's standards it was a remarkably small bureaucracy for such a population, but certainly a very effective one.

Entry to the elite category of the administration as a *guan* official could be achieved in a number of ways. One could enter on the grounds of one's father's or grandfather's noble title, or through hereditary privilege if one's father or grandfather had held office of the fifth rank or above. One could become eligible through service in the guards. Sons of officials of the sixth rank and above could be assigned as guards attached to the emperor, the heir apparent or a royal prince. After thirteen years in service such guards were examined, and the most successful candidates were placed on the roll of officials. Those with a responsibility for the management of public funds could also be considered for an official post. In this way sons of those who practised business could gain access to officialdom, and again this diluted the aristocratic stranglehold on the court.

Those employed as *liuwai-guan* could gain promotion to the *guan* class as well. The 'outside the current' officers who held positions such as clerks, secretaries, writers and messengers had their own hierarchy within the membership. Staff could apply for promotion within the class, generally after three years' service. After eight years' service officers could apply for promotion to become a *guan*. This proved to be a popular course of career development, suggesting that the civil service in Tang China was indeed firmly established. In 657 some 1400 such upgradings are recorded and the figure rose to around 2000 in 729. However, such officials obviously came from undistinguished non-aristocratic backgrounds, and the most important and influential posts in the bureaucracy were denied them. Finally, entry to the official class was determined by examination. Embodied in the structure and style of the Confucian civil service examination was the whole gamut of the social and political ethic of China and it is, therefore, a feature worthy of investigation.

Before a candidate could sit for the examination he had to be selected and recommended by an appropriate authority. There were but two such authorities: the Directorate of the State University (in the capital) and the relevant local prefecture authority. Those debarred from consideration included relatives of serious criminals and sons of merchants and artisans, who were considered to be 'morally tainted' in their primary pursuit of profit.

The Directorate of the State University controlled a small number of separate higher schools in the capital, each of which had a specified quota of students. Three of these schools provided the classical curriculum which was required for entry into officialdom. While this elite education system developed and expanded through the dynasty, these schools, the *Guozi* (School for the Sons of State), the *Taixue* (Superior School) and the *Simen xue* (School of the Four Gates) remained the mainstays of the system. The number of students was limited; in Gao Zu's reign a mere three hundred are recorded, but this increased to two thousand in Tai Zong's succeeding reign. Two further schools, the *Hongwen guan* (College for the Development of Literature) and the *Chongwen guan* (College for the Veneration of Literature) were established for the exclusive use of sons of the imperial family and the very highest-ranking ministers. As such, these students had hereditary access to the official class and were not necessarily expected to display exceptional abilities; they had only to attain a 'moderate standard' in their studies.

In the four corners of the actual tomb chambers of deceased royalty and nobility were placed pottery models of fearsome guardian figures or lokopalas, *secular versions of the Guardian Kings of Buddhism. Their task was to ensure the protection of the deceased and to ward off any evil spirits. This outstanding, 103cm (40in) high example has a characteristically demonic appearance. It was in such figures that the Tang craftsmen seemed to enjoy complete freedom of imaginative display.*

內艾安府庫充實
而四夷未賓制度
多闕上方欲用文
武求之如弗及始
以蒲輪迎枚生見
主父而歎息群士
慕嚮異人並出卜
式技於芻牧羊
擢於賈豎衛青奮
於奴僕日磾出
於降虜斯亦曩時
版築飯牛之明已
漢之得人於茲為
盛儒雅則公孫
董仲舒兒寬篤行
則石建石慶質直
則汲黯卜式推賢
則韓安國鄭當時
定令則趙禹張湯
文章則司馬遷相
如滑稽則東方朔
枚皋應對則嚴助
朱買臣曆數則唐
都洛下閎協律則

ABOVE *The painted and gilded doors of an audience hall in Beijing's Forbidden City convey a sense of the mystery and intrigue that went on behind them. But it was also in these quiet courtyards of the Inner Palace that the imperial family, ministers and officials would pursue their studies and exercise their scholarly skills.*

LEFT *The consummate Confucian expression 'The Eulogy of Ni Kuan', written by the early Tang dynasty scholar-minister Chu Suiliang, noted for both the* kaishu *(official) and* lishu *(clerical) scripts. His calligraphy was described by the Tang critic Zhang Huaiguan as having 'the grace and delicacy of a beautiful woman'.*

Candidates from the regions were presented on the recommendation of their prefectural authority. Each prefecture had a set quota of candidates, depending upon the size of the region. In overall terms, the regions submitted far more candidates than the capital (in the mid-eighth century some two to three thousand against the capital's four hundred or so), but the metropolitan candidates' success rate was very much greater. The standards of teaching were higher in the city; those privileged candidates, furthermore, had access to officials and the hierarchy, scholars of note, the central aristocracy and all manner of people who could assist and influence them. Records of statistics bear out the metropolitan bias; in 670 one in eleven of the regional candidates was successful; in 682 a mere one in fifty-five and in 704 just one in forty-one.

In political, social and cultural terms, China in the Tang dynasty was, therefore, very much a metropolitan culture. The vast majority of the population were peasant farmers, but the arbiters of taste, style, and political and social life were the elite of the cosmopolitan capital, Changan.

Candidates were examined primarily on the Confucian classics, although knowledge and understanding of other fundamentals of the Chinese ethic, such as Taoism, was also required. The purpose of the examinations was to identify those candidates with a proper feeling for the Chinese style and the Confucian ethic and, of course, the capacity to formalize that knowledge and understanding into a framework for political and social administration. There were also special subject examinations for such syllabuses as law, mathematics and philology, but these were considered peripheral.

The two examinations of real importance were the *mingqing* and the *jinshi*, which early in the dynasty were very nearly indistinguishable. In reforms carried out in 681 these two examinations were redefined and the pattern was set for the remainder of the dynasty. The *mingqing* or 'clear understanding' (of the classics) placed greater emphasis upon a close knowledge of the classic canons. The *jinshi* or 'promoted scholar' examination placed greater emphasis on literary skills and qualities of judgement in politics and the affairs of government. As such, the *jinshi* examination was considered by far the more important of the two, particularly in the eighth century, by which time the professional bureaucrat class was in the ascendancy.

In general, the pass rate for these examinations was low – distressingly low for those who sat for them. The standards set were extremely high and, furthermore, it was not practicable to pass candidates that the system could not absorb into the lofty realms of officialdom, although it does seem that some successful candidates were left unemployed. Records indicate that a success rate of between five per cent and ten per cent was the norm in the Tang period for the *mingqing* and a mere two per cent for the *jinshi*.

It is worth reflecting briefly on the nature of the official class. The ideal official was regarded as a man of 'broad humanistic culture' imbued with ethical standards, with understanding of and regard for the political and social norms and, of course, a full knowledge of the classics. He was, therefore, a man who could make sound judgements on any issue. Technical and specialized knowledge and skills were not necessarily admired, as such specifics might obscure, interrupt or divert the mind from the overall view. It was that capacity for a detached appreciation of the whole which distinguished the true Confucian scholar. At the same time, more specialized pursuits that fell wholeheartedly within the Confucian-scholar ethic, such as calligraphy and poetry, were greatly admired. Some of the values that the traditional Confucian scholar cherished and aspired to may be glimpsed in an extract from the diary of the fourteen-year-old Pu Yi, written after his abdication as the very last emperor of imperial China, long after the Tang dynasty, in 1918:

27th: Fine. Rose at four, wrote out eighteen sheets of character Prosperity in a large hand. Classes at eight. Read *Analects* [Confucius], *Zhou Ritual, Record of*

Ritual, and Tang poetry . . . . Listened to tutor Zhen lecture on the *General Chronological History with Comments by the Emperor Qianlong* (1736–95). Finished eating at 9.30. Read *Zuo Commentary, Guliang Commentary*, heard tutor Zhu on the *Explanations of the Great Learning*, wrote couplets. Lessons finished at eleven, went to pay respect to four High Consorts. Johnston [the diplomat Sir Reginald Johnston who gave English lessons] did not come today as he had mild flu, so returned to the Heart Nurture Palace and wrote out thirty more sheets of the characters Prosperity and Longevity. Read papers, ate at four, bed at six. Read *Anthology of Ancient Literature* in bed: very interesting.[7]

A typical day in the life of a youthful Confucianist!

The life-style and aspirations of the Chinese people were, of course, bound to alter during the course of a dynasty as enduring as the Tang. The motivation for any change, albeit firmly within the broadly outlined ethic of the Confucian ideal, was the tenor of life at the court. After the consolidating and immensely successful reign of the Emperor Tai Zong (reigned 626–49) the Tang dynasty entered a less stable phase. First there was some dissent concerning the succession, as the nominated heir apparent, Li Chengqian, adopted a somewhat 'wayward' life-style and a liking for 'barbaric' Turkish customs, including dress. Eventually Tai Zong's ninth son, Li Zhi, was chosen to succeed as the Emperor Gao Zong (reigned 649–83), despite some reservations on the part of his father.

Unfortunately Tai Zong's fears were realized, for as the histories record, when Gao Zong should have been providing imperial guidance and leadership in debate he would merely 'fold his hands and do nothing'. Worse still, Gao Zong brought to the scene of the imperial court one of the most remarkable women in China's history, having abandoned his first, and childless, consort. A certain Wu Zhao, previously a lowly consort to Gao Zong's father, had in accordance with tradition left the imperial harem upon the death of the Emperor, shaved her head and entered a Buddhist monastery. On a visit to that monastery, the new Emperor recognized and recalled her. The extraordinary Wu Zhao was a woman of beauty, determination, intelligence and unscrupulous political opportunism. Gao Zong opened the door of imperial China to Wu Zhao and thereby changed the course of the history of the Tang dynasty.

Having been recalled to the court early in the decade beginning in 650, she had by 655 been elevated to the status of empress. In order to remove any threat to her new power and status, Wu disposed of the previous empress, Wang, and a concubine, Xiao Shufei, by having their arms and legs cut off and leaving them to die in a wine vat. By the mid 670s the weak Gao Zong was so overawed by Wu Zhao and her powerful infiltration of government that he nearly abdicated in her favour. As the eleventh-century Song historian and minister Sima Guang wrote: 'The great powers of the empire all devolved upon the Empress. Promotion and demotion, life and death, were settled by her word. The Emperor sat with folded hands.'[8]

With the death of Gao Zong in 683, all effective power devolved upon the Empress Wu. Two weak emperors maintained an ineffective Li line: Zhong Zong, who reigned for six weeks, followed by Rui Zong (reigned 684–90). In 690 Empress Wu usurped the throne and for the first and only time in the history of China the Mandate of Heaven was accepted by a woman. Since Wu Zhao was not a member of the royal Li family she was at liberty to change the name of the dynasty and this she did, naming it the Zhao dynasty. The essential structure of the administration remained the same, but there occurred a substantial change in attitude. Without the widespread support of the traditional establishment and aristocratic families, Empress Wu had to rely more heavily on the appointed officials. Entry to officialdom through the examination system, rather than through hereditary means, increased substantially under her rule, setting the pattern for subsequent administrations in imperial China. The influence of an educated elite at the court brought a new flair and imagination to the administration.

ABOVE *The tomb mound and memorial stele of Li Shimin, Emperor Tai Zong, the son of the founder of the Tang dynasty. Construction of the tomb began in 636 and was completed thirteen years later. The entire burial complex, which is at Zhaoling to the north-west of Xian, has a 60km (37 mile) perimeter and contains no less than 167 tombs of members of the royal family and prominent officials.*

LEFT *The upper section of the massive 7m (23ft) high memorial stele surmounted by nine entwined dragons at the joint tomb of Emperor Gao Zong and his consort Empress Wu at Qianling, 85km (53 miles) north-west of Xian. It is known as the 'Tablet With No Inscription' as the principal dedication was never made – perhaps because of Empress Wu's last words: 'Let later generations comment on my achievements and errors,' which of course none felt inclined to do. There are, however, forty-two brief inscriptions dating from the Song dynasty and later, praising the Qianling tomb.*

However, the influence of the Empress was the paramount feature and that influence was not always good. Her extraordinary energies were devoted not only to governing the empire but also to pursuing all manner of intrigues and tensions. Her granting of totally unjustifiable favours, such as appointing one of her lovers, a thoroughly undistinguished cosmetic and aphrodisiac pedlar, to be chief abbot of the country's most prestigious Buddhist temple, the White Horse Temple (Bai-ma-si) in Loyang, caused inevitable friction. Considerable power in the hands of inept officials undermined the integrity of government. Fortunately for history, her more enduring contributions, such as the limited democratization of government, were essentially beneficial, while her more wicked and whimsical actions had little lasting effect except to provide historians with an endless source of outrageous stories.

The succession to Empress Wu returned the Li family line to the imperial throne and thus the name of the Tang dynasty was restored. These were unsettled times and the restoration of the two brief-serving emperors, Zhong Zong and Rui Zong, did little to re-establish confidence. These weaknesses were resolved with Li Longji's accession to the throne in 712 as the Emperor Xuan Zong. Xuan Zong not only reigned as the longest-serving emperor of the Tang (712–56), he also restored the status of the dynasty to the glory of Tai Zong's reign. Confidence was fully restored and Chinese armies were once again victorious across the steppes and deserts of Central Asia as far as the Pamirs. The economy was stable, Buddhism flourished, and the arts were as gregarious and active as ever.

In the mid-eighth century it seemed China merely had to stretch out her arms in order to embrace the world. The capital, Changan, thronged with traders, merchants, emissaries, monks and entertainers from all parts of the Tang empire and far beyond, and could justifiably lay claim to being the most cosmopolitan city in the world.

Xuan Zong's reign represented the peak of Tang achievement and that peak also witnessed the beginning of a decline that culminated in the end of the dynasty a century and a half later. As is always the case, a combination of factors led to the decline in the ultimate fortunes of the Tang, but certainly a significant turning point was the defeat of the Tang armies by a Thai state in Yunnan in 751, followed by their defeat at the hands of the Arabs at Talas in the far western regions of the empire beyond the Tarim basin. This defeat prefaced the loss of Chinese control over Central Asia and somehow undermined the total confidence that had previously emanated from Changan.

The Emperor Xuan Zong, too, was past the peak of his powers by the mid-eighth century, and when he fell under the sway of a beautiful young consort of one of his sons, the notorious Yang Guifei, the once mighty Emperor gave himself over to the pursuit of frivolous pleasure. Without that supreme and inspiring focal point the empire descended into a state of profound uncertainty. The practical problems that had previously been hidden under the cloak of imperial confidence quickly began to surface.

It is an extraordinary fact of history in China that any cracks or weaknesses at the heart of the court always seemed to compound quickly into disaster. The Emperor's association with Yang Guifei paved the way for an ambitious general, An Lushan, to be admitted into the inner court. Within a short space of time he had some 200,000 troops under his command. In 755, An Lushan sought complete power and captured both the eastern capital of Loyang and the principal capital of Changan. The Emperor and Yang Guifei fled to Sichuan province, a flight immortalized in a famous painting, but the imperial troops accompanying the royal pair, dissatisfied by this sad turn of events, forced the Emperor to execute the person whom they felt to have been responsible for the débâcle, Yang Guifei. Totally broken and disgraced, the Emperor Xuan Zong abdicated the throne and one of the greatest periods in the history of China came to an unhappy conclusion.

Political intrigue apart, the real problems facing the Tang administration were the strains placed upon the imperial coffers caused by the need to maintain a huge and expensive court, an administration that spread throughout the empire and an equally substantial military establishment. These all imposed considerable and increasing demands on the revenue-raising departments of government. The basic revenue-raising commodity was land and it was therefore in the best interests of the government to keep as much land as possible in the hands of the tax-paying members of the community, above all the peasant farmers. A rudimentary system of land distribution which sought to maximize potential tax revenue had been established by the Northern Wei in the fifth century, and it was essentially this practice that was inherited by the Tang after further refinements by the preceding Sui dynasty.

Under this system, known as the 'equal field' distribution of land, every able-bodied male between the ages of twenty-one and fifty-nine was entitled to one hundred *mu* (approximately five and a half hectares/fourteen acres) of land of which twenty *mu* (approximately one hectare/two and three quarter acres) could be permanently owned and handed down, the remainder to be handed back upon the death of the holder to the state for redistribution. In return the holder was obliged to pay taxes of a fixed amount of grain, silk or hemp and to give his services twenty days a year in corvée labour. Obviously, the high-ranking families of the aristocratic and official classes had, or were provided with, extensive estates outside the 'equal field' system. But it was not always in the interests of the court coffers to have the empire divided up into these massive estates as they were essentially non-productive as far as taxes were concerned and, furthermore, employed potential peasant farmers who, if brought into the 'equal field' system, would become tax-payers. Thus, although large aristocratic estates were not abolished, the creation of further such estates was severely restricted. The 'equal field' system of land distribution survived throughout the Tang dynasty but was probably at its most effective during Xuan Zong's reign when the administration was tight and controls over the build-up of extensive land-holdings were determined. The tax administration, too, was at the height of its effectiveness at this time, with over two and a half million households registered, and thus liable to tax, in the year 742. This was, however, undermined upon the collapse of Xuan Zong's rule.

Despite these severe setbacks in the mid-eighth century, Tang China continued to enjoy at least another century of comparative peace and prosperity. The years from the middle of the eighth century to the second half of the ninth century were neither as glamorous nor as confident as the heady days of the mid-seventh and early eighth centuries. Reforms and refinements in the government and the tax system in particular, including a fundamental alteration to the latter which transferred tax liability from the man as holder of the land to the land itself, assured that central government maintained a general control over the officers of state. But it was a gradually decreasing level of control.

Behind this outward appearance of calm there was emerging another group of actors on the court stage who were to play a significant role in the declining years of the dynasty. During Xuan Zong's reign, contrary though it may seem to the general style of those successful years, the eunuchs began to exercise power and influence at the court. The role of the eunuch in China's imperial history has always been one of intrigue, guile, ruthlessness and often cruelty. Since their original role was simply to act as servants and since that continued to be their essential *raison d'être*, the degree of power and influence they exercised throughout China's imperial history until the early twentieth century is extraordinary. Castration had for many years been a form of punishment in China but just how and when eunuchs came to serve at the court is unclear. Certainly they were employed in their primary function, as overseers of the imperial harem, as early as the Zhou dynasty, and during the Han dynasty (206 BC–AD 220) the eunuchs had established influential power bases within the court.

As men of no education, insubstantial background and with no aristocratic or official support, it was thought they posed no threat, and the eunuchs thus became trusted confidants of empresses and even emperors. As such they undermined the authority of the official class, and since it was the Confucian scholar-officials who wrote the histories, eunuchs have been roundly and consistently condemned as perverse and mischievous sycophants in formal histories. As early as the late Zhou dynasty the *Shi Jing* (*Classic of Songs*) likens the eunuchs to interfering ladies:

> A woman with a long tongue
> Is a stepping-stone to disorder.
> Disorder does not come down from Heaven –
> It is produced by women.
> Those from whom come no lessons, no instruction,
> Are women and eunuchs.

In the later Tang dynasty the eunuchs' rise to power began with their gradual involvement in the day-to-day administration of the court. As messengers between the emperor and his ministers they became privy to the most important confidential matters of policy and they gradually assumed control over the palace guards and certain military establishments at the capital. The ever-increasing eunuch influence at court, the friction between the officials and the eunuchs and the gradual alienation of the provincial administrations combined to fragment the credibility of the imperial court. Regional aristocratic families and military commanders increasingly ignored their commitments to Changan, as did many thousands of tax-paying land-holders. Finally, with the fabric of Tang society breaking up, China's traditional foes, the Mongols, the Turks and the Tibetans, took the opportunity of exploiting her weaknesses in military adventures.

While it would be inaccurate to place the emphasis of blame for the final collapse of centralized government upon the eunuchs, it seems appropriate to conclude any review of the administration of Tang China with a discussion of the group that was central to its downfall. As is so often the case, it was the weaknesses within, indeed within the most sacrosanct chambers of the imperial household where the eunuchs exercised their influence, that were at the root of the demise of the Tang.

What is extraordinary, but so characteristic of the enduring qualities of Chinese social structure, is that the roundly criticized eunuchs continued to exercise the same kind of power and influence in subsequent dynasties. There are no precise records of how many were serving at the Tang court but they must have numbered in the thousands, and in the Ming dynasty (1368–1644) the eunuchs' strength at court reached 100,000. Even after the revolution that ended imperial rule in China in 1911, the eunuchs remained. According to a list of 1922, over a thousand eunuchs were still in the service of the imperial household and of the households of various remnants of the imperial line, including the former Emperor Pu Yi. His account of the lingering role of the eunuch in his childhood could have been written in the Tang dynasty:

> The duties of the eunuchs were very extensive. In addition to being in attendance at all hours, carrying umbrellas and stoves, and other such jobs, their tasks, according to the *Palace Regulations*, included the following: transmitting Imperial edicts, leading officials to audiences and receiving memorials, handling official documents of the various offices of the Household Department, receiving money and grain sent by treasuries outside the palace, and keeping a fire watch; looking after the books of the library, the antiques, calligraphy, paintings, clothing, fowling-pieces, bows and arrows; keeping the ancient bronzes, the *objets de vertu*, the yellow girdles granted to meritorious officials, and fresh and dried fruit; fetching the Imperial Physicians to attend in the various palaces, and obtaining the materials used in the palace by outside builders; burning

An anonymous painting of possibly Tang dynasty date, The Flight of the Emperor Ming Huang to Shu, *illustrates the Emperor Xuan Zong (also known as Ming Huang) and his entourage on their journey to Sichuan when fleeing from the An Lushan rebellion in 755. The painting is executed in the so-called Tang 'blue and green' landscape style, dominated by fairy-tale pinnacles, winding valleys and wispy clouds.*

incense before the records and precepts of the emperor's ancestors, their portraits, and the gods; checking the comings and goings of the officials of various departments; keeping the registers of the attendance of the Hanlin academicians and of the watches of the officers' sovereign; flogging offending eunuchs and serving women; feeding the various living creatures in the palace; sweeping the palace buildings and keeping the gardens tidy; checking the accuracy of the chiming clocks; cutting the emperor's hair; preparing medicine; singing opera; reciting classics and burning incense as Taoist monks in the City Temple; becoming lamas in the Yung Ho Kung [Palace of Eternal Harmony], as substitutes for the emperor and many other duties . . . .[9]

A series of massive rebellions in north China that began in 874 signalled the opening shots of the campaign that finally brought the Tang dynasty to its close. Dissatisfaction with a corrupt administration and increasing impoverishment among the people stimulated widespread popular uprisings, and regional commanders and leading aristocratic family groups exploited the absence of strong central government and declared virtual autonomy. It was one of those regional commanders, Zhu Wen, who in 904, while in the service of the Tang Emperor Zhao Zong (reigned 888–904), had him and all his sons except one assassinated. The one surviving son became the puppet emperor of Zhu Wen until 906, when he abdicated and left the way clear for Zhu to establish his short-lived Liang dynasty which heralded six decades of upheaval and disorder.

Like all the great dynastic cycles the Tang had run its course and, characteristically, made its final exit not in an explosion of civil war or natural disaster, but as an eroded and crumbling edifice.

3
THE MIND BEHIND
Confucianism, Taoism and Buddhism

The gregarious Tang dynasty, with an eager appetite for new styles, ideas, fashions and flavours from the outer reaches of the empire and beyond, nonetheless had a firm base in traditional Chinese values and philosophy. At the very heart of these values was Confucianism.

By the time the Tang dynasty was founded, Confucianism was already twelve centuries old. During those centuries it had undergone embellishment, reinterpretation and refinement, and had accepted and absorbed influences from other philosophies and religions, including Taoism and Buddhism, but its central theme concerning the principles of human conduct had remained intact. That Confucianism survived as the basic criterion for the well-ordered life in China for over 2000 years is testimony to its tenacity. But it is also testimony to its flexibility and capacity, as a wide-ranging and never too specific or dogmatic philosophy, to adapt to changing times, values and circumstances. To a lesser extent, this quality of philosophic elasticity also ensured the longevity of Buddhism in China. As a foreign ideology, Buddhism achieved a reluctant acceptance and that really occurred only after the faith had acquired a mantle of Chinese identity in its interpretation. This involved broadening the doctrine from being one of pure ideological religion to one which embodied a more general religious philosophy. In this slight but significant transformation, elements of traditional Chinese thought from both Confucian and Taoist schools were absorbed into the Buddhist religion. Thus eventually all three principal schools of Chinese thought and philosophy influenced one another.

This process was well under way by the time of the Tang dynasty, when all three schools, and indeed a number of others, were flourishing. In many respects it was the enlightened attitude of the Tang and its receptiveness to new ideas that allowed those cross-currents to develop. Another inevitable, and valuable, consequence of this freedom of thought was the development and emergence of variant schools as offshoots of the mainstream traditions.

Although Confucianism is often seen as a religion, it bears no resemblance to our usual concept of religion as a structured faith with a complex hierarchy of deities and icons. Nor is it a philosophy which seeks to establish the whys and wherefores of our existence. Confucianism has never sought to explain why Man exists. Rather, it has sought to establish an order within which human society could operate. Fundamental to that order is a recognition of two essential precepts: that society requires a hierarchy and that certain rights and responsibilities between human beings exist and should be forever acknowledged.

The Buddhist guardian king Vaisravana, a late Tang dynasty painting said to have come from the temples at Kucha, to the west of Turfan, along the northern route of the Silk Road. This is a classic example of the region's unique blend of Chinese and Central Asian traditions.

39

The emotional, ethical and imaginative concerns and aspirations of Man that were, in Western societies, more generally expressed through a formal religion were absorbed into the great philosophical debate in China. Philosophy in China was always concerned with practical matters, with Man in society and the structure and organization of that society. The sense of hierarchy has, therefore, always been a significant factor in social organization. The aptly termed 'golden age of Chinese thought' was the period of turmoil, conflict and virtual anarchy that occurred towards the end of the Bronze Age in the Eastern Zhou period (sixth to fifth centuries BC). It was at this time, during the Spring and Autumn Annals and Warring States periods, when established and long-accepted notions of social and political structure were proving inadequate to the purpose of sustaining the empire, that an extraordinary range of statesmen, scholars and philosophers began to question even the most sacred of institutions in their search for a new order. These great debates consolidated the enduring association between philosophy and government in underlining the need for a humanistic social ethic to serve as the basis for good government.

Prior to the upheavals of the Eastern Zhou period, social and philosophical traditions in Bronze Age China had been based on the concept of a patriarchal society in which the chain of authority descended directly from the emperor, so that the whole society resembled an enlarged family structure. Religious and ceremonial activities reflected the importance of the family-clan structure in recognizing ancestor worship as their central theme. That same simple structure also imposed a kind of natural authoritarianism on Chinese society, as clearly defined chains of command tend to in any society or community. So well grounded were such ideals in the Chinese way of life that they too were reflected in later philosophies, especially Confucianism, in which authority and responsibility were recognized as vital to the structure of an ordered society.

The structure of early society in China was founded upon the recognition of certain basic rules of conduct and responsibility known as *li*, literally translated as ritual, ceremony or proper conduct. Such refinements concerning the details of life related only to that small section of society subject to official stratification, the ruling hierarchy. This was acknowledged at the outset in the earliest surviving compendium of the philosophy of conduct, the *Li Ji* (*Record of Ritual*), thus:

> The *li* does not extend down to the common people; punishments do not extend up to the great officers.[1]

Although the *Li Ji* describes ritual as a necessary prerequisite to the maintenance of order in society through the definition of the hierarchy and the rights and duties associated with such positions, it was Confucius who identified the specific value of such practices. He emphasized that the multitude of ceremonies and rituals that gave tangible form to *li* were the external form of inner qualities, values and disciplines. Thus the maintenance of proper ceremony was essential to the maintenance of proper values.

Confucius was born in the eastern state of Lu, in present-day Shandong province, in 551 BC. He travelled widely throughout the empire, like so many other such philosopher-statesmen, seeking a suitable government post. All the while he taught and discussed, gathering a coterie of students and followers, but he never found a post in any administration that he considered appropriate to his status and wisdom. His teachings have been preserved in the *Analects* and take the form of a series of brief dialogues – questions and the Master's answers. Confucius, like his philosopher colleagues, expressed little interest in religion and metaphysics; his attentions were focussed solely on earthly problems. To an enquiry about death he replied: 'Not yet understanding life, how can I understand death?'

Much of Confucian thought is embodied in the great writings of the ancients, known as the classics, those same works that formed the basis of the syllabus for the

A portrait of Confucius carved on a stone stele now in the Forest of Steles in the Shaanxi Provincial Museum in Xian. Originally carved in the Tai Zong reign of the Tang dynasty, the inscription on the reverse side was re-cut in the early years of the Song dynasty in the second half of the tenth century.

official examinations in Tang times. The four ancient classics which subsequently became the basis of the Confucian ethic are the *Yi Jing* (*Book of Changes*), the *Shu Jing* (*Book of Documents*), the *Shi Jing* (*Book of Odes*) and the *Li Ji* (*Record of Ritual*). The *Yi Jing* comments upon the ancient divinations practised in the Shang dynasty; the *Shu Jing* is a compendium of speeches, announcements and counsels given by the great figures of the distant past such as the mythical rulers Yao and Shun; the *Shi Jing* is an anthology of some three hundred poems, principally of early Zhou date; and the *Li Ji* comments on a wide range of subjects, from matters of broad philosophical interest to the conduct of everyday affairs.

What all these books had in common was a basic interest in the debate relating to the conduct of human affairs on earth. To these four books must be added a later work entitled the *Chun Qiu* (*Spring and Autumn Annals*), a brief chronicle of events in Lu, Confucius's home state, from 722 to 481 BC. All of these were written before the time of the Master, although the *Chun Qiu* has often been ascribed to him. History and tradition have assigned to Confucius the role of transmitter and editor of, as well as commentator on, these classics, and of course through the intervention of Confucius the values they express became embodied in the Confucian ethic. Confucius summarized the values held in the classics in his conversations which were recorded in the form of the *Analects*. These too, therefore,

The stone stele and burial mound at the tomb of Confucius, located to the north of the Temple to Confucius at Qufu in Shandong province. The tomb itself is marked by a modest mound a little over 4m (13ft) in height; the stele was erected in 1443 with an inscription which reads 'tomb of the Prince Wen Xuan, very accomplished and very holy'. Wen Xuan was the posthumous title given to Confucius during the Tang dynasty.

became absorbed into the philosophy and syllabus of the aspiring officials of the Tang dynasty.

Possibly the main reason for Confucius's eventual success was that the essential humanism central to his thinking triumphed over the superstition, mysticism and often simple cynicism that characterized other contemporary schools of thought. Furthermore, the specific interpretation of humanistic ideals could be adjusted to suit changing conditions and values of the day. Confucianism identified the qualities that human society should aspire to and stressed Man's inherent capacity for virtue. However, in Confucius's view the true qualities and virtues of Man could be revealed only through education: 'By nature men are pretty much alike; it is learning and practice that sets them apart.'[2]

The most significant Confucian virtues were those of *ren* (human-heartedness) and *yi* (righteousness). *Ren* may be generally translated as 'humanity', 'love', 'goodness'. It is that supreme capacity for excellence, benevolence and altruism that, according to the Master, exists in everyone. Once, when asked about *ren*, Confucius replied: 'It is to love all men.' In another way the Confucians saw *ren* as a greater wisdom, a foundation upon which Man could adjust and adapt to all conditions: 'Those who are without virtue cannot abide long either in a condition of poverty and hardship, or in a condition of enjoyment. The virtuous rest in virtue, the wise desire virtue.'[3]

The quality of *yi* (righteousness) describes that quality which the Confucians believed to exist with similar universality in mankind. *Yi* defines Man's instinctive assessment of what is essentially 'wrong'. One of Confucius's most influential followers, Mencius, said: '. . . the feeling of shame and dislike is the beginning of righteousness.' Confucius believed that everyone was born with these instincts, but it was only through learning that they could be transformed into realistic and tangible values.

The outward manifestations of these qualities were found in the ritual known as *li* and in the notion of *wen*, meaning culture, which represented, in a variant form, those same qualities of depth, maturity and integrity. Through learning and the proper application of his humanitarian instincts, Man would be morally, intellectually and materially equipped to rule and counsel. The formalization of these qualities in the ritual of *li* was thought by the Confucians to be an essential ingredient of good government. Of course, the highest ideals of Confucianism were moderated by the passage of time, changing values and the influence of other theories, but the Confucian ethic, the idea of the necessity for a responsible and benevolent hierarchy, and the stress laid upon the value of right education were sustained through the centuries.

Of the sundry divergent schools of Confucian thought that exerted some influence upon that style of Confucianism which became synonymous with the Chinese tradition, the most important were those of the thinkers Mo Zi (*c*. 470–391 BC), Mencius (*c*. 372–289 BC) and Xun Zi (born *c*.312 BC).

Mo Zi may originally have been a close follower of Confucius's thought, for the basis of his thesis was the same humanitarian approach as that of the Master. However, he eventually adopted a position that was critical of the Confucianists for their lack of recognition of the role of Heaven and the spiritual powers in the determination of an ideal form for human society. Mo Zi's philosophy was to follow the true way of Heaven; he believed that all people are equal and that the way to harmony on Earth is through universal love. Within such a Utopian concept, Mo Zi saw the Confucian order of ritual and hierarchy as a divisive element and considered it unnecessary and wasteful. He carried the Confucian notion of inherent goodness to its logical, if extreme, conclusion. Although his views did not become absorbed into the mainstream of Confucian thought, they represent a significant offshoot and above all another point of reference for the continuing debate on the Confucian ethic.

Mo Zi recognized that the standards of Heaven had to be transmitted to the

The layout of the Temple to Confucius: a rubbing taken from a stele in the Forest of Steles, Xian. First built a few years after his death in 479 BC, the temple was expanded in the Tang dynasty, then again in the Song and Ming dynasties. The present temple was built in 1724 although many of the stone carvings, engravings and steles are of much earlier date.

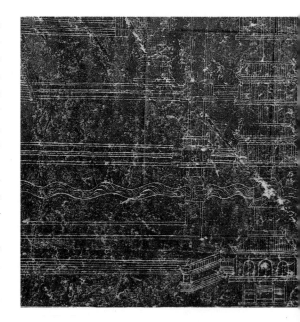

people through a proper sense of righteousness. That quality, although inherent in Man, had to be revealed through training and teaching:

> Now a standard is never given by a subordinate to a superior, it is always given by a superior to a subordinate. Hence the common people may not take any standard they please; there are the scholars to give them the standard. The scholars may not take any standard they please; there are ministers to give them the standard. The ministers may not take any standard they please; there are the feudal lords to give them the standard. The feudal lords may not take any standard; there are the three ministers to give them the standard. The three ministers may not take any standard they please; there is the Son of Heaven to give them the standard. The Son of Heaven may not take any standard he pleases; there is Heaven to give him the standard.[4]

The innate sense of hierarchy which Mo Zi sought to eschew is quite apparent in this extract from his principal writing, the *Mo Zi*. It is perhaps only the identity of 'Heaven' as the source of that sense of righteousness that distinguishes Mo Zi from the Confucianists. Whereas they saw the sense of righteousness as something fundamental to the human race, Mo Zi saw it as a quality inspired by powers beyond Man:

> . . . be sure to do what Heaven desires and forsake what Heaven abominates. Now what does Heaven desire and what does Heaven abominate? Heaven desires righteousness and abominates unrighteousness. How do we know that is so? Because righteousness is the proper standard. How do we know righteousness is the proper standard? Because when righteousness prevails in the world, there is order; when righteousness ceases to prevail in the world, there is chaos . . . .[5]

The brook at the Temple to Confucius identified in the rubbing, which still flows today between marble parapets and under gently arching bridges in the southern section of the temple near the main gateway. It is said that some of the pine trees in this area of the temple date from the Han dynasty, and they must therefore be nearly 2000 years old.

The Great Goose Pagoda in Xian, built in 652 – a rare example of original Tang dynasty architecture. The seven-storeyed 60m (200ft) high pagoda was built by the monk Xuan Zang after his return from his 17-year-long sojourn in India; in it he established a translation workshop to interpret the vast library of Buddhist texts and sutras that he had brought with him from the source of Buddhism.

In the history of Confucian thought, Mo Zi's Utopian ideal of universal love has been overshadowed by the contribution of Confucius's closest follower, Mencius, who lived some two centuries after the Master. Like Confucius, Mencius was a wandering scholar-philosopher who became more a teacher than a practising official. Fundamental to his philosophy was his belief in the essential goodness of Man. Like Confucius, Mencius believed that Man's inherent virtue could be transformed into something useful only through learning. Unlike Confucius, however, he believed that people were born morally equal and that, through education and learning, everyone could acquire those qualities of virtue, discrimination and wisdom that the purest Confucians considered the preserve of those born to the elite. Mencius thus had a very considerable influence upon the Confucian doctrine in proposing that the qualities of leadership were inherent in everyone, and that influence was particularly felt in the Tang dynasty, when the selection of officials through the examination system, as opposed to through exclusively hereditary means, was widespread.

Like Confucius, Mencius dwelt at length on the qualities of leadership. *Ren*, benevolence, was the quality above all others that identified the true king. It was a quality that would be manifest in the ruler's perpetual care and concern for his subjects:

He who, using force, makes a pretence to benevolence is the leader of princes . . . . He who, using virtue, practises benevolence is the sovereign of the empire . . . . When one by force subdues men, they do not submit to him in heart. They submit because their strength is not adequate to resist. When one subdues men by virtue, in their hearts' core they are pleased, and sincerely submit, as was the case with the seventy disciples in their submission to Confucius. What is said in the Book of Poetry:

'From the west, from the east,
From the south, from the north,
There was not one who thought of refusing submission,'
is an example of this.[6]

The emperor's benevolence was extended to the people through the officials, *junzi*, who displayed that same quality in the exercise of their duties. In the system of things Chinese, society was divided into two broad classes: the *junzi* (literally, 'ruler's son'), and the *xiaoren* ('small man'). This distinction represents a notion of upper and lower classes which parallels the duality that underlines all aspects of Chinese thought. The successful *junzi* had to display the same quality of benevolence that characterized the emperor's style. Such division in Chinese society provided not only a social framework but, just as significantly, an ethical framework in which greater human virtue accrued to the upper echelons of society.

This ethical framework, which formed such an integral part of the socio-political structure of life in China, was the great and enduring contribution of Confucian thought. It is a vital aspect of the Confucian principle that order and harmony in the world can be secured only by Man acting in harmony with the forces and powers of nature and the universe. Implicit in this world view was a total acceptance of that order and a belief that people must adjust to it in unison. A significant consequence of this acceptance was that diversity of opinion and reaction was deplored, which also contributed to the unity and stability of that society.

The development of Confucian thought was influenced too by the contribution of Xun Zi, whose interpretation constituted what is often referred to as the 'realist' school of Confucianism. Unlike Mencius, who believed in the essential goodness of Man, Xun Zi believed that Man is essentially evil. Central to Xun Zi's thinking was his belief that the fallibilities of human nature could be overcome only through a strict and formal education, and this led inevitably to a belief in and acceptance of a dogmatic and systematic social structure, which was enshrined in *li*, ritual:

Man's nature is evil; goodness is the result of conscious activity. The nature of Man is such that he is born with a fondness for profit. If he indulges this fondness, it will lead him into wrangling and strife, and all sense of courtesy and humility will disappear. He is born with feelings of envy and hate, and if he indulges these, they will lead him into violence and crime, and all sense of loyalty and good faith will disappear. Man is born with the desires of the eyes and ears, with a fondness for beautiful sights and sounds. If he indulges these, they will lead him into licence and wantonness, and all ritual principles and correct forms will be lost. Hence, any man who follows his nature and indulges his emotions will inevitably become involved in wrangling and strife, will violate the forms and rules of society, and will end as a criminal. Therefore, Man must first be transformed by the instructions of a teacher and guided by ritual principles, and only then will he be able to observe the dictates of courtesy and humility, obey the forms and rules of society, and achieve order. It is obvious from this, then, that Man's nature is evil, and that his goodness is the result of conscious activity.[7]

From this it would seem that the prospect for mankind is rather bleak, yet in principle Xun Zi adheres to the general Confucian philosophy, differing only in his basic premises regarding the essential nature of Man and his even more rigid application of order and hierarchy in the social structure. Xun Zi certainly echoed the Confucian ideal in his views on the need for the 'superior man' to be a generalist as opposed to a specialist:

The farmer is well versed in the work of the fields, but he cannot become a director of agriculture. The merchant is well versed in the ways of the market, but he cannot become the director of commerce. The artisan is well versed in the process of manufacture, but he cannot become a director of crafts. Yet there are men who, though they possess none of these three skills, are still able to fill the offices that direct them. This is not because they are well versed in the facts, but because they are well versed in the Way. He who is well versed in the facts alone will treat each fact as a fact and no more. He who is well versed in the Way will unify his treatment of the facts. Hence, the gentleman finds a basis for unity in the Way and on this basis examines and compares the facts. Since he has unity of the Way as his basis, his approach will be correct; and since he examines and compares the facts, his perception will be clear. With thinking that is based upon a clear perception, he is able to control all things.[8]

Xun Zi, in the annals of Chinese philosophy, is allied closely to the Legalist School. Legalist thought was very much a product of its day, the tumultuous times of the late Warring States period, when the reunification of a fragmented empire could have been achieved only by the imposition of such an authoritarian and doctrinaire philosophy. That reunification was achieved under the dogmatic rule of Qin Shihuang and his Legalist advisers. However, as an independent ideology, Legalism had little to offer in the longer term and was quickly superseded by a truer and more benevolent form of Confucian government in the succeeding Han dynasty. Yet the brief experience of Legalism during the shortlived Qin dynasty (221–206 BC) was not without influence upon the subsequent style of government in China. In particular, the structure of the centralized government achieved by Qin Shihuang had an enduring influence upon the style and flavour of the administration in later dynasties, including the Tang dynasty, whose leaders aspired to that same concept of centralism.

The Confucian ethic was indisputably the single most important factor in the determination of the style of life in Tang China and the values held by its people. While in specific terms it was a code that had greater relevance to the higher echelons of society, its values permeated the humblest of family structures. At this

The spirit of ancient Chinese philosophy and attitude lives on in this calligraphy by the contemporary calligrapher Li Jinxue, who lives in the city of Loyang. The two characters read 'Mo' and 'Zhuang' – Mo for Mo Zi, the great fifth-century-BC disciple of Confucius, and Zhuang for Zhuang Zi, the fourth-century-BC Taoist philosopher.

level the Confucian concept of filial piety dominated and determined the strength of family unity: respect for one's parents and for the elderly are attitudes as Confucian as they are traditionally Chinese. In the Confucian tradition, the word *wen*, meaning 'culture', came more specifically to refer to the pattern of cultural values. If one were to seek a single element to embody the Confucian ideals of benevolence, goodness, propriety, order, harmony, learning and wisdom, it would be *wen*. That quality informed the spirit of human conduct in the administration of the Tang dynasty. As a leading writer, historian and scholar of the Tang dynasty, Xiao Yingshi (706–58), wrote: 'How perfect is *wen*! It is a great unifying principle to which Heaven and Man unite in responding, and through which the purpose of names and schedules is preserved.'[9]

While Confucianism was the guiding philosophy in practical affairs in Tang China, it was not a doctrine that wholly fulfilled Man's natural curiosity in otherworldly affairs. Nor indeed did Confucianism cater to Man's natural tendency to believe in the supernatural. Taoism fulfilled that role as the only native Chinese philosophy that verged on being a religion, in the accepted Western sense. Like Confucianism, Taoism was born out of the chaos and uncertainty of the late Zhou period, a time unrivalled in the history of China for its range and activity in philosophical and intellectual thought. In the atmosphere of free-ranging thought of the Tang dynasty, Taoism played a significant role in the formation and expression of the values and aspirations of the Chinese people, particularly those outside imperial and official circles.

Taoism dismissed the ethical concerns of Confucianism and concentrated on nature and the forces of the universe. The Taoist believed that Man was a mere extension of nature, and that nature was the material manifestation of the forces of the universe. To seek the true nature of Man, therefore, one must look to the sources, to nature and beyond. Whereas the Confucians saw harmony in a contrived human order, the Taoist view was that harmony could be achieved only by Man subconsciously and subjectively playing out his role as merely a part of the great design of the universe. Within the natural order, Man was a small part, of no greater importance than any other.

The Taoists believed that ultimate truth was a vastly more powerful force than the Confucian order. That truth was embodied in the 'Tao', literally translated as the 'Way'. Fundamental to that belief was the notion that whereas the material extensions to the self-generating forces of nature and the universe, Man included, were mortal and in a constant state of change, the Tao was constant. The Tao was the combination of natural forces and processes that established the essentially unchanging but superficially ever-evolving pattern of the grand design. The Tao was the harmony that drew the pattern.

The logic and reason of a contrived human order were alien to Taoist thought. Seeing in essential natural order the ultimate guiding force, the Taoists felt that the interference of Man could only serve to disturb the harmony. Thus Man should not seek to change things, but should subject himself to the overwhelming conditions and forces of the natural order. The greatest of the early Taoist philosophers, Zhuang Zi (*c.* 369–286 BC), emphasizes the point in characteristically succinct and eccentric style thus:

An unglazed pottery model of a lady seated reading a book. This calm and serene figure seems to embody the scholarly Confucian ideal, but of particular interest is the book, since bound volumes, familiar in Western and Central Asia in pre-Tang times, only became popular in China during the Tang dynasty.

The duck's legs are short, but if we try to lengthen them, the duck will feel pain. The crane's legs are long, but if we try to shorten them, the crane will feel grief. Therefore we are not to amputate what is by nature long, nor to lengthen what is by nature short.[10]

The obvious corollary to the acceptance of the philosophy of the Way is that values and conditions imposed by Man are irrelevant. In fact the Taoists believed that considerations such as *ren* (benevolence) and *yi* (righteousness) were a positive impediment to consciousness of the Way:

When the great Tao is abandoned, benevolence and righteousness arise.
When intellect emerges, the great fabrication begins.
When families are in discord, dutiful sons appear.
When the State falls into anarchy, loyal subjects are to be found.
Banish wisdom, discard knowledge, and the people will benefit
a hundredfold.
Banish benevolence, get rid of righteousness, and the people will return
to find piety and kindness.
Banish ingenuity, eschew profit, and there will be no more
thieves and brigands.[11]

The Confucian ethic and its attendant structures within society were the very
antithesis of the Taoist ideal. The followers of Taoism's traditional founder, Lao Zi
(born 604 BC), its greatest writers Zhuang Zi and Lie Zi (probably third century
AD) therefore eschewed public life and certainly any kind of service within an
administration.

The Confucian emphasis upon learning and knowledge was a very real hind-
rance to subjective awareness of the Way. Zhuang Zi again said: 'Our life is

limited, but knowledge is limitless. To pursue the limitless by means of the limited is dangerous. To strive for knowledge in spite of that is dangerous indeed!'[12] To the Taoists the only knowledge that was of value, in that it could lead to the Way, was intuitive knowledge. The true Taoist would never soil his hands or the purity of his mind in the affairs of state. Stories of the great Taoists' unworldly conduct abound and have contributed greatly to the romantic eccentricity that seems to characterize the philosophy. Zhuang Zi's refusal to become involved in politics and worldly matters when offered a ministerial position with the State of Chu is typical:

> He told the messenger . . . 'A thousand pounds of gold is a substantial reward, and ministerial rank is an honourable position. But have you alone not seen the ox used for the sacrifice outside the city walls? After being fattened up for several years, it is decked out in embroidered trappings and led into the great temple. At that moment, even if it wanted to change into an orphan piglet, it would be quite impossible. Go away! Do not defile me! I would rather enjoy myself by frolicking in the mire than be haltered by the ruler of a State. To the end of my life I will never take office. Thus I will remain free to follow my own inclinations.'[13]

Such attitudes gave rise to a notion that, in many ways, is the all-encompassing basic rule for Taoism, that of *wu-wei*. It is a phrase that may be conveniently translated as 'non-action'. The principal Taoist text, the *Dao De Jing* (*Tao Te-ching*) says: 'The Tao never acts, yet there is nothing it does not do.' This concept recognizes the ultimate and inevitable forces of the Way and implies that harmony between the Way and mankind can be achieved only through spontaneous and subjective reaction on the part of Man. Conscious action or intervention by Man will serve only to interrupt the pattern and thus bring about discord.

The purity of the Taoist philosophy and its opposition to the notion of structure in society presented problems for its survival. While the Taoist philosophy contributed much to the development of original and imaginative thought in literature and art, and to a very real awareness of the natural world, it suffered from the lack of the kind of formal identity that it eschewed. A consequence of this was the emergence of a Taoist religion (*Dao Jiao*), as opposed to the Taoist philosophy (*Dao Jia*), in which the aspirations of the philosophy were debased into a crude form concerned principally with means of gaining immortality. In this respect the semi-formal Taoist religion was the very antithesis of the philosophy, for what could be more unnatural than seeking to deny the inevitability of death?

Nevertheless, the religion, which developed during the third to fourth centuries AD, became a popular cult religion in which Lao Zi was deified as the God of Immortality with his legendary attendants, the Eight Immortals, and an abundance of beguiling and colourful imagery involving Taoist Paradises, Elixirs of Immortality and associated exotic beliefs. Popular religious Taoism soon became far removed from its cogent and visionary philosophic origins.

Taoism, both philosophic and religious, was much favoured in the Tang dynasty, as the ruling Li family claimed descendancy from Lao Zi, the philosophy's reputed founder and author of the Taoist classic, the *Dao De Jing*. So accepted as a founding element in the Chinese style and ethic was Taoism that the official examinations included both the *Dao De Jing* and the *Zhuang Zi* in the Confucian-dominated syllabus. The attraction that this nature-mystic way of thought would have had for the relatively free-thinking people of Tang China is clear. However, the impact of the semi-formal Taoist religion was perhaps even greater. By the early eighth century, there were over 1600 active monasteries, and religious Taoism had acquired a pantheon of gods and deities, scriptures and monastic orders. Indeed, in its structure and concepts of iconographic hierarchy, it was not unlike its main rival, Buddhism.

Approximately 70km (45 miles) east of Turfan lie the Buddhist temples of Bezeklik, most of which were originally built in the open and joined by wooden porches. Others were carved into the living rock in the manner of cave temples. The height of activity at Bezeklik, on the evidence of surviving wall paintings, was the Tang dynasty when the Silk Road trade brought travellers, merchants and missionaries to the temples in search of sanctuary and spiritual comfort. Today they are still difficult to reach, for the monks endeavoured, even here in the desert wastelands of Chinese Central Asia, to build their temples as far away as possbile from the real and profane world.

Part of this growth was inspired by a reaction against the even more emphatic spread of Buddhism, the foreign faith. The authorities went to some lengths to establish Taoism as something more than popular myth. In the founding reign of the Tang dynasty, Lao Zi was honoured with the title Taishang Xuanguan Huangdi, 'Most High Emperor of Mystic Origin', a title ranked above those accorded both Confucius and the Buddha. The time of greatest imperial support for Taoism was the reign of Xuan Zong in the eighth century, when the Emperor even wrote a commentary to the *Dao De Jing* – a great honour. However, characteristically, he wrote commentaries to Confucian and Buddhist texts as well just to ensure proper distribution of imperial favour and hedge the ideological bets.

The form of religious Taoism that evolved during the three to four centuries preceding the Tang, and which was the basis for Tang religious Taoism, was based on three doctrines: immortality on Earth, internal and external alchemy (which embodied commitment to the natural order of things) and the notion that the span of one's life might be determined by conduct. The probability of longevity and the possibility of immortality as rewards for appropriate conduct naturally had widespread appeal – far greater appeal among the general populace than the studied elitism of Confucianism or the hierarchical ideology of the Buddhist religion.

The philosophic background to this trinity of religious Taoist doctrines was enshrined in a work of the late third to early fourth century AD entitled the *Baopu Zi (The Philosopher Who Embraces Simplicity)*. Although the work embodied earlier writings, and while the detailed format of later religious Taoism was further refined and amended by later, particularly fifth-century, writers, this text may be regarded as the basic source of religious Taoism in the Tang period. The author, Ge Hong, is reputed to have met with some success in his own quest for longevity; at the age of eighty-one he was described as having 'a complexion like that of a child'! Like many of the early Taoists seeking truth and purity, Ge lived the life of a virtual hermit shut up in his house; it is recorded that he often 'had a hard job to push his own way through the brambles which choked up the path to his door'.[14]

Ge Hong's *Baopu Zi* describes the three doctrines at some length. The section on immortality emphasizes the irregularities within the regular overall pattern of existence, offering the possibility of longevity even within a finite life:

> Life and death, beginning and end, are indeed the great laws of the universe. Yet the similarities and differences of things are not uniform. Some are this way and some are that. Tens of thousands of varieties are in constant change and transformation, strange and without any definite pattern. Whether things are this way or that and whether they are regular or irregular in their essential and subsidiary aspects cannot be reduced to uniformity. There are many who say that whatever has a beginning must have an end. But it is not in accord with the principle of existence to muddle things together and try to make them all the same. People say that things are bound to grow in the summer, and yet the shepherd's-purse and the water-chestnut wilt. People say that plants are bound to wither in the winter, and yet the bamboo and the cypress flourish. People say whatever has a beginning will have an end, and yet Heaven and Earth are unending. People say whatever is born will die, and yet the tortoise and the crane live forever. When the *yang* is at its height, it should be hot, and yet the summer is not without cool days. When the *yin* reaches its limit, it should be cold, and yet even a severe winter is not without its warm periods . . . .[15]

The thesis on internal and external alchemy was based on the idea that the immortals nourished their bodies and prolonged their lives through sciences associated with the occult. It proposed that the absorption of such spirits, often taken in the form of herbs and elixirs, would prevent detrimental ailments from entering the body and causing physical breakdown and death. The *Baopu Zi* again:

> I have investigated and read books on the nourishment of human nature and collected formulas for everlasting existence. Those I have read number thousands of volumes. They all consider reconverted cinnabar (turned into mercury) and gold fluid to be the most important . . . . If these two medicines are eaten, they will strengthen our bodies and therefore enable us not to grow old or die . . . .[16]

In addition, breathing exercises and sundry sexual activities, the 'art of the chamber', were considered by the Taoists as aids to longevity.

On the third doctrine, that a good and natural life leads to a prolonged one, the *Baopu Zi* has this to say:

> The doctrine of retribution expounded here resembles in some ways the Buddhist conception of karma. Although it is difficult to establish any definite historical connection between the two, it should be remembered that at this time Buddhism and Taoism borrowed extensively from each other and shared many of the same concepts and terminology.[17]

The same source elaborates upon the theme in describing such qualities as goodness, humanity, benevolence (*ren*) towards not only human beings but all aspects of the natural world if one is to seek immortality. Such a notion relates to Buddhist ideology, which in turn absorbed the karma theory from the Hindu religion. Both Buddhist and Confucian notions are hinted at in this extract from the *Baopu Zi*:

The Small Goose Pagoda, located to the south of the present city wall of Xian, was built in 706 in the grounds of the Da Qing Fu temple. The original buildings were known as the Da Xian Fu temple and constructed by Empress Wu in honour of Emperor Gao Zong in 684, the year of his death. In 690 the temple was restored, given the name Da Qing Fu, and with 200 resident monks because a prosperous and well-known Buddhist establishment.

Their [those who seek immortality] hearts must treat others as they treat themselves, and extend their humaneness (*ren*) even to insects. They must rejoice in the good fortune of men and pity their suffering, relieve the destitute and save the poor. Their hands must never injure life, and their mouths must never encourage evil. They must consider the success and failure of others as their own. They must not regard themselves highly, nor praise themselves. They must not envy those superior to them, nor flatter dangerous and evil-minded people. In this way they may become virtuous and blessed by Heaven; they may be successful in whatever they do, and may hope to become immortal.[18]

The third major force in the development and formation of Chinese thought and philosophy in the Tang dynasty was Buddhism. No other foreign ideology and system of thought that achieved any kind of presence in China, including Nestorian Christianity, Manichaeism, Islam and Zoroastrianism (all of which appeared during the Tang dynasty) and Catholicism (in later times), made such a lasting impact. So totally absorbed did Buddhism become that it acquired a unique and distinctive Chinese form, embodying notions, themes, styles and terminology from the native Confucian and Taoist schools.

Many, and often apocryphal, stories surround the arrival of Buddhism in China. With some certainty it can be said that the faith was introduced to the Middle Kingdom in the first century AD, during the Eastern Han period, at a time when the confident, successful and expansive Confucian empire of the Han had passed its zenith but had not really entered a perceptible decline. Nevertheless, the dynasty itself had been challenged by the Wang Mang interregnum (AD 8–23), when the throne had been usurped, supposedly in the interests of restoring the pure Confucian ideal; thus there must have been some question regarding the viability and durability of the Confucian ethic as a practical basis for government and society. It was in this atmosphere of basic cultural assurance, tinged with a slight lack of confidence in the real world, that Buddhism came to China.

In both conceptual and ideological terms the Buddhist style was as different from the Chinese style as it would have been possible to imagine at the time. The Chinese style, enshrined in historical awareness and the Confucian ethic, was worldly and practical. Buddhism was full of vivid imagery and notions concerning the supernatural and reincarnation. Furthermore, the religion came to China expressed in a grammatical and alphabetical language totally alien to the ideographic Chinese system. One would have expected such a faith to have little chance of success in the sophisticated, structured and ideologically mature society of Han China. It is not surprising, therefore, that Buddhism was at first regarded as a somewhat wayward form of Taoism. Indeed, familiar Taoist terminology was frequently employed in the interpretation of Buddhist texts in China, thus forming from the outset some relationship between the two ideologies and sowing the seeds for a distinctive Chinese style of Buddhism.

The collapse of the Han dynasty in the early third century AD and the subsequent sense of insecurity, loss of faith and social disruption provided Buddhism with a unique opportunity. In the succeeding years the weaknesses of a series of shortlived imperial houses allowed monastic communities to assert both authority and autonomy. The first centuries of Buddhist growth in China, during the Northern and Southern Dynasties period before reunification by the Sui in AD 581, are characterized by distinctive theological developments in the north and south. During these centuries, the north was under non-Chinese rule, and the south was ruled by a series of lesser Chinese dynasties. While Buddhism was accepted in the south, it never received imperial favour and patronage, and the Buddhist communities which emerged there did so without a sense of unity and without any semblance of real authority. Unlike these independent southern monastic communities, those in the north found it convenient and indeed necessary to align themselves with the ruling house of the day. Thus the monks frequently became political and military advisers to the government, thereby establishing a relationship between religion and state that was to become a feature of Chinese Buddhism in the fifth and sixth centuries, and above all in the Tang dynasty. In addition, it must be noted that the rulers of north China, as non-Chinese, were more receptive to a foreign ideology than were the Chinese rulers of the south.

This fundamental difference in the establishment of the faith is reflected in contrasting doctrinal developments. In the north the constant flow of monks and followers to and from China, as well as the commercial and military contacts along the Silk Road, established and maintained close connections with the Central Asian and Indian centres of Buddhism. In addition, much of the population of north China, including many of the monks, were of Central Asian and even Indian origin. Thus the northern monastic communities, whose translations of the *sutras* or Buddhist scriptures were of great significance in the formation of early Chinese Buddhism, represented an extension of Central Asian and Indian ideals.

The fall of the great northern capitals of Loyang and Changan to the Xiungnu, a Turkish-speaking Tartar people, in the early fourth century signalled the departure of large numbers of Chinese, particularly members of the literati and official classes, from the north to south of the Yangtze. Under their aegis, a distinctly Chinese variant of Buddhism evolved during the southern Eastern Jin dynasty (AD 317–420), one which was strongly influenced by learned and literary Chinese. There was great emphasis on theoretical matters, and traditional Chinese thought coloured the interpretation of Buddhist texts. In this way, the technique of *geyi* was established, whereby familiar Taoist or traditional Chinese terminology was used

to explain Buddhist ideas. One famous exponent of *geyi* was the monk Hui Yuan (AD 337–416) who was well versed in both Taoist and Confucian literature:

> Once some guests listened to his lectures, and questioned him about his theory of reality. Though the discussion continued back and forth for some time, they became increasingly doubtful and bewildered. Thereupon Hui Yuan quoted ideas from the *Zhuang Zi* [the Taoist text] that belonged to the same category and in this way the sceptics came to understand.[19]

This method of transposition is illustrated by the Chinese interpretation of the most important southern text of the time, the *Prajnaparamita* (*Perfection of Wisdom*) *Sutra*, of which several versions and translations existed in both north and south China. The principal teaching of this *sutra* concerned *sunyata* (emptiness). According to this text, *dharmas*, elements of reality, existed only in relation to other things. Thus their true nature was *sunya* (void). *Sunyata* was equated with the Taoist concept of *wu-wei*, 'non-action' or 'non-being'.

Meanwhile, in the north, it is recorded that as early as AD 299 over half the population of the Changan region was of non-Chinese origin. This proportion must surely have been maintained, if not increased, with the Xiungnu takeover a few years later. It was during this early period of non-Chinese rule that Buddhist monks found it rewarding to align themselves to the ruling houses. The most significant outcome of this close relationship between religion and state was intermittent imperial patronage. It was in such circumstances that, during the Later Zhao dynasty (AD 329–52), the monk Fo Tudeng was proclaimed 'a great jewel of the state'. Such patronage initiated the making of images of the Buddha, thereby inspiring a whole new sculptural tradition in China, one that was to attain fulfilment in the Tang dynasty. The great cave temples and their impressive sculptures at Yungang and Longmen are lasting testimony to the imperial patronage of Buddhism in China.

A signal event in the history of Chinese Buddhism was the arrival in Changan in 401 of Kumarajiva, a monk from Kucha in Central Asia. Kumarajiva's major contribution was the organization of the mass of Buddhist material that had already been translated. He applied a method new to China: illustrating and organizing Buddhist doctrine through the leading principle of a single *sutra*, in this case the *Prajnaparamita*. In doing this, he reaffirmed the basic direction of the

development of the Buddhist faith in China, towards Mahayana Buddhism.

The Mahayana doctrine, which advocates working to help attain salvation for all sentient beings, grew out of dissatisfaction with the narrowness of Hinayana Buddhism – the original form of Buddhism. Now found only in the form of Theravada (doctrine of the elders, or canonical Buddhism), Hinayana is essentially a discipline for personal salvation by the individual on his own behalf; the term means 'Lesser Vehicle', while Mahayana means 'Greater Vehicle'.

It was at about this time that the first important Chinese pilgrim, Fa Xian, left China for India in search of the holy law. These were still tentative days for Buddhism in China, with contacts in the hands of a few dedicated monks and a large number of lay travellers and merchants. Fa Xian's departure for India inaugurated a large movement of Chinese monks to India in pursuit of their studies.

In the early fifth century the overland route to Central Asia, and thence to India and beyond, passed through Northern Liang dynasty territory in Gansu province. The capital, Liangzhou, therefore became a flourishing centre for Buddhist activities, a sanctuary for monks travelling to and from China and a refuge for those fleeing from areas of conflict in the north. Also in Liang territory were the Dunhuang cave temples, the earliest of which date from the middle of the fourth century but which reached their apogee in the Tang dynasty, when Western iconographic and artistic styles were first influenced by Chinese ideals. The leading monk at Liangzhou in the early fifth century was Dharmakshema who was responsible for a translation of the *Mahaparinirvana Sutra*, which became the basic

text of the Nirvana School in China – a school of widespread popularity in the Tang dynasty. The Nirvana School promoted the discussions that abounded concerning the concepts of 'sudden' (Mahayana) enlightenment and 'gradual' (Hinayana) enlightenment. Such discussions were popular in the two centuries preceding the Tang dynasty in both north and south China. The general acceptance of the 'sudden' enlightenment approach, a concept which, of course, could more readily be assimilated with native Taoist ideals, confirmed the Mahayana nature of Chinese Buddhism.

When the Toba Turkic people established the Northern Wei dynasty in AD 386, thereby initiating a period of relative calm and unity in north China that lasted until the early sixth century, they encountered a kind of institutionalized religion that was already involved with governmental processes. Thus the first emperor, Tai Zi (reigned 386–409), ordered his armies not to violate any Buddhist establishments. Having invited monks to serve as advisers, the Northern Wei rulers confirmed and developed the association between religion and state. Buddhism became the adopted religion of the Toba people, received official patronage and was set for a period of total acceptance and establishment across north China. However, under pressure from Confucian and Taoist advisers, the third emperor, Shi Zi (reigned 425–51), turned his attention to consolidating and expanding the empire. In 439, Northern Liang territory fell to the Toba and with it the extensive Buddhist establishments there. Among the persistent resisters to the invaders were the monks, and some 3000 were taken as prisoners to metropolitan China. Such an enormous influx, together with the already existing Buddhist communities, convinced the Emperor of the necessity to restrict religious activity. This led to the persecution of Buddhists in 446, the wholesale destruction of temples, images and monasteries, and the forced return to lay life or execution of the monks.

A gradual relaxation of these stern measures against Buddhism followed and the next emperor, Wen Cheng (reigned 452–66), actively supported the religion. Major Buddhist temple constructions, including the renowned Yungang cave temples, were commissioned. Symbolic of the new attitude was the appointment of Tan Yao as chief monk, and his period of office, some twenty years, witnessed the first period of consistent and fruitful imperial patronage – a pattern which continued well into the sixth century.

Southern China in the fifth and sixth centuries witnessed similar but less dramatic developments. The relationship between religion and state had always been more tenuous in the south, since it relied principally upon the common interests of the Buddhist clergy and the ruling classes, whereas in the north Buddhism had become both a tool and an extension of the government.

At the end of the Northern Wei dynasty, north China became divided under the shortlived Western and Eastern Wei dynasties. Their territories were subsequently taken over by the Northern Zhou (in 557) and the Northern Qi (in 550) respectively. Buddhism was adopted and encouraged by the eastern dynasties and enjoyed the now familiar pattern of state support and patronage.

During the sixth century there was a gradual change in the nature of Buddhist doctrine in China. Early in the century and before, the historical Buddha, Sakyamuni, and the future Buddha, Maitreya, were the most popular deities because of a traditional interest in the *Lotus Sutra*. By the end of the sixth century, Amitabha Buddha and the Bodhisattva Avalokitesvara had become the most popular deities, reflecting an increased interest in the Pure Land School with its promise of Paradise. These highly appealing doctrinal developments formed the basis of Chinese Buddhism during its apogee in the Tang dynasty.

Thus in the three centuries prior to the founding of the Tang dynasty, Buddhism was established in China. The attraction of the Paradise theme emerged as the basis for the expansion of the doctrine in the Tang, and the religion-state relationship that was forged by the Northern Wei became the structural foundation upon which the religion flourished in the Tang.

The increasing popularity of the Paradise Sutras *in the mid to late Tang dynasty brought Bodhisattva figures to prominence in Buddhist iconography. Of these the Bodhisattva Guanyin, Avalokitesvara, such as this carved marble example of late Tang dynasty date, was the most popular, eventually becoming known as the Goddess of Mercy.*

4
THOUGHT, PHILOSOPHY AND ATTITUDE IN THE TANG

While the foundations of Tang philosophy were provided by the well-established traditions of Confucianism, Taoism and Buddhism, an increasingly expansive vision, assisted by fresh ideas and values from distant lands and a growing interest in the natural world, created an atmosphere of unparalleled intellectual vitality and curiosity. More than at any other time in history Chinese artists, philosophers and poets were inspired directly by the environment rather than by the ritualistic framework of the social order.

Probably the greatest influence on Chinese thought and attitude in the Tang was the overwhelming belief in the destiny of China. This belief was founded on an unshakeable confidence in the Chinese way – a confidence that inspired the arbiters of Chinese taste and style to look beyond the Middle Kingdom.

Confucianism remained the essential core of philosophical debate in Tang China. It was expedient for successive emperors to wholeheartedly support Confucianism, for in doing so they were supporting the system that maintained their own powers and authority. As an ethical code, Confucianism did not substantially alter during the Tang, but merely became further reinforced in the social system. As it became increasingly important as the ethical backbone of the administration and the basis of the educational system, so it inspired an extraordinary literary output. Essay-writing, poetry, *belles-lettres*, the writing of histories, and of course calligraphy, achieved new heights under the auspices of benevolent Confucianism.

The most significant influence upon the dissemination of information through the written word, and one of infinite value to the general heightening of awareness of varying philosophies and attitudes, was the development of wood-block printing. Rubbings on soft, thin paper taken from stone carvings had been an accepted practice in Han times, but it was not until the early Tang dynasty that full-page wood-block printing developed. By 868 the technique had developed enough to make possible the printing of a whole Buddhist *sutra*, and by the late Tang the Chinese classics were available in printed form.

It was not until nearly the end of the Tang dynasty that any pressures were brought to bear upon the seemingly impregnable Confucian hierarchy. External pressures, from the early ninth century onwards, inspired the conservatism that was dramatically expressed in the anti-Buddhist purges. These events led to a resurgence of interest in traditional Confucian values, which formed the basis for the Neo-Confucian movement. This movement opposed the anti-political notions of Taoism and the foreign anti-social aspects of Buddhism, for both these traditions tended to undermine Confucian authority.

The town of Yueyang in Hunan province is chiefly known for the tower, originally built in the third century, that stands above the west gate in the old city walls. Here the poet Li Bo and his colleagues would meet, drink, discuss and hold poetry competitions.

However, new directions in Chinese thought had inevitably enriched the original form of pure Confucianism of late Zhou times that the Neo-Confucianists sought to restore. The late Tang development was, therefore, not so much the restoration of ancient ideals as a revitalization of the tradition. Neo-Confucian terminology and its concern with metaphysics show the influence of parallel philosophies, in particular Taoism and the *Chan* (or, in Japanese, Zen) form of Buddhism. Nonetheless, Neo-Confucianism at heart remained a realistic, practical and worldly ethic, and never allowed Taoist notions of immortality or Buddhist concepts of salvation and the after-life to become part of its doctrine.

One product of the Neo-Confucian movement, characteristic of the growing reaction within intellectual circles to the foreign style of the Tang, was the *guwen* (literally 'ancient literary style') movement, which advocated the reform of prose from the euphemistic and decorative style so appropriate to the Tang character to a simpler, more concise style modelled on Zhou and Han writings.

Han Yu (786–842), generally acknowledged as the principal figure in Tang Neo-Confucianism, illustrates the direction of the movement and, in particular, how the language of Confucianism had been coloured by the parallel theologies of Taoism and Buddhism, in this excerpt from his *Yuan Dao* (*The True Way*):

To love universally is called humanity [*ren*]; to apply this in a proper manner is called righteousness [*yi*]. The operation of these is the Way [*Tao*], and its inner power [*de*] is that it is self-sufficient, requiring nothing from outside itself. Humanity and righteousness are fixed principles, but the Way and its inner power are speculative concepts. Thus we have the way of the gentleman and the way of the small man, and both good and evil power. Lao Zi made light of humanity and righteousness, but he did not thereby abolish them. His view was narrow, like that of a man who sits at the bottom of a well and looks up at the sky, saying: 'The sky is small.' This does not mean that the sky is really small. Lao Zi understood humanity and righteousness in only a very limited way and therefore it is natural that he should belittle them. What he called the Way was only the Way as he saw it, and not what I call the Way; what he called inner power was only power as he saw it, and not what I call inner power. What I call

BELOW *The beauty, elegance and eloquence of the scholarly Tang style is expressed in Huai Su's autobiography, written in 777. Born in 725 in Changsha with the family name Qian, he left to become a monk; Huai Su is his religious name. Known to be something of an eccentric, Huai once said that he had obtained the special secrets of the sages of the cursive style of writing – the style of this calligraphy and for which he was famous. One of the many anecdotes about Huai recounts that when young he was too poor to buy paper and so planted banana trees in order to obtain their leaves, on which he would be able to write.*

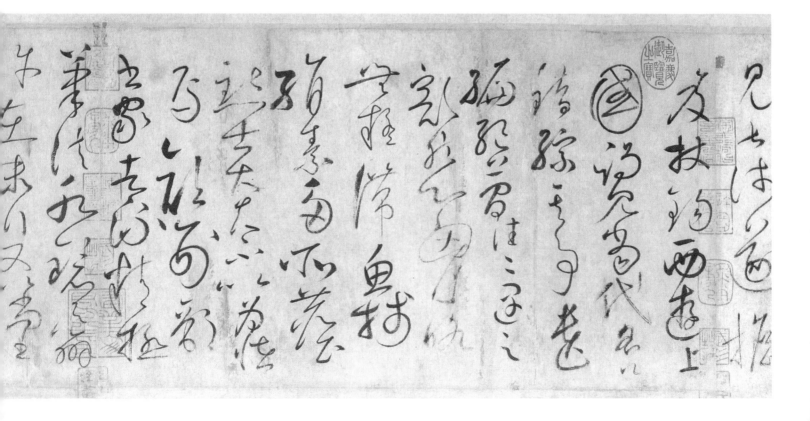

RIGHT *The world's earliest surviving printed book: a wood-block printed version of the* Diamond Sutra *dated to 868 that was found at the Dunhuang Buddhist cave temples. The* sutra *consists of individual sheets of printed text and a frontispiece illustrating the Buddha surrounded by acolytes and disciples stuck on to a backing in the manner of a handscroll with a total length of an amazing 5m (16ft). The colophon reads: 'Reverently made for universal free distribution by Wang Jie on behalf of his parents on the fifteenth of the fourth moon of the ninth year of Xian Tong,' which corresponds to 11 May 868.*

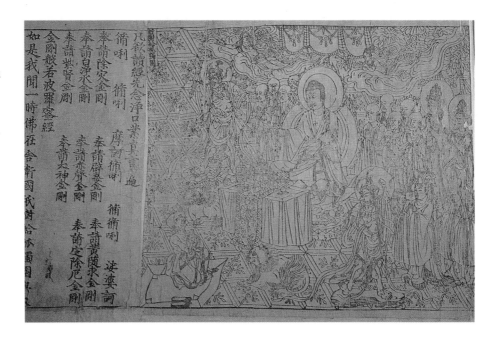

ABOVE *Art for the scholar's desk: a glazed pottery water-dropper in the form of a mandarin duck. Water contained in the vessel was gently shaken on to the ink stone and mixed with ink cake or stick to produce the ink.*

the Way and inner power are a combination of humanity and righteousness and this is the definition accepted by the world at large. But what Lao Zi called the Way and power are stripped of humanity and righteousness and represent only the private view of one individual . . . .[1]

This is an evident mixture of Confucian and Taoist terminology, though the general direction of the philosophy is strongly Confucian. The noticeable development which distinguishes Neo-Confucianism from Confucianism in its original form is the introduction of metaphysical considerations concerning 'inner powers' and 'the Way', in contrast to the more purely ethical and structural nature of its predecessor.

While traditional agnostic and non-theistic Confucianism continued to strengthen its position as the ideological framework of Chinese society, the less worldly and more colourful Taoism and Buddhism were in many ways more attractive propositions. Indeed the majority of the Tang emperors, who publicly supported Confucianism, were privately inclined to Taoism and Buddhism.

It has been noted that Taoism developed from a taut, if romantic, philosophy to a popular cult religion in the Tang. The search for immortality was the central theme of popular religious Taoism in the Tang. Even emperors were tempted into the search for the Taoist elixir of never-ending life.

However, in the development of thought and attitude perhaps the most significant contribution of Taoism was its role in focussing a general anti-foreign feeling. At a time when China was so gregarious this may seem strange, but from the mid-eighth century on, increasing problems in the border regions combined with the extraordinary power and influence of Buddhism to cause a backlash. There emerged an increasing tendency to resist outside forces and return to native themes and ideals. This culminated in the anti-Buddhist purges of 841–5, and while the Buddhist establishment was the particular focus of the onslaught, it escalated into a campaign against many foreign ideals and establishments. It was effectively a purge of all non-Chinese elements, something of a nationalistic cleansing process not unlike the much later Boxer Rebellion and the recent Cultural Revolution. Foreign ideals which had so enriched the great metropolitan communities at Changan and Loyang in the north and Canton in the south were, Buddhism excepted, virtually extinguished in China in the mid-ninth century.

Earlier in the dynasty the influence of such religions as Nestorian Christianity, Zoroastrianism, Islam and Judaism had contributed to a broadening of the intellectual and philosophical horizons in Tang China. None were established to the extent of having a significant Chinese following, but their presence permeated higher levels of Chinese society and certainly attracted the curiosity of the Tang intelligentsia.

Nestorian Christianity arrived in China from Mesopotamia and was active through missionary work until its final expulsion by the Mongols in the fourteenth century, though it was relatively insignificant after the mid-ninth century. According to the inscription on a monument erected in Changan in 781, Nestorian Christianity was brought to China at the time of Emperor Tai Zong in 635, by a missionary named A Loben from Daqin – the 'Near East'. It is even recorded that the missionary bearing this distant and unfamiliar creed was greeted with some warmth by the Emperor, who ordered translations of sacred books to be made and permitted the construction of a temple for the Nestorians in Changan. This religion of mixed Christian and Near Eastern beliefs had been established in Persia just two centuries earlier under the guidance of a Syrian ecclesiastic named Nestorius, the Patriarch of Constantinople from 428 to 431, who had later fallen out with the Church of Rome and the Byzantine Empire. The fact that such a faith could find immediate if limited favour in Tang China is a measure of the vogue for things foreign and exotic in the Middle Kingdom.

Zoroastrianism was another religion brought to China by travellers along the Silk Road from Sassanid Persia. Zoroaster, or Zarathustra, is thought to have lived

The Sheng Xin Lou or 'Tower of Introspection' inside the Great Mosque at Xian that was founded in 742 in the Tang dynasty although the present buildings largely date from the Ming dynasty. Outwardly like any other Chinese temple, the mosque complex is truly Islamic in detail, with minarets, prayer halls and Arabic as well as Chinese inscriptions throughout.

in north-east Iran in the sixth century BC and was the founder of the religion that bore his name. Zoroastrianism, or Mazdaism (from the Wise Lord, Ahura Mazda, regarded by Zoroaster as God), developed in a more formal sense in the early Sassanian period (AD 224–651). The cult of fire worship was central to the rites of Zoroastrianism, the eternal flame representing the divine essence and source of life. It was a mixture of Iranian folklore and Christian principles. Zoroastrians saw the world as a permanent battleground for the forces of good and evil, but believed that good was sure to triumph. As such, therefore, the religion developed a strong ethical order which, together with its dualism, paralleling the *yin-yang* dualism in Chinese thought, may have assisted its limited acceptance in Tang dynasty China.

The seventh century witnessed the arrival in Changan of yet another Christian-based Middle-Eastern religion, Manichaeism. A hybrid faith with a mixture of Iranian mythology and Christian cosmological ideology, in which the underlying factor was the Christian principle of distinguishing between good (light) and evil (dark), Manichaeism was founded in the third century by a high-born Persian, Mani. Like Nestorian Christianity and Zoroastrianism, it failed to gain a firm foothold in China; nevertheless the presence of these Western theologies, together with their trader or merchant adherents, missionaries and acolytes, brought to the Tang capital, and to a lesser extent to other major cities, a breadth of intellectual experience that eventually became very much a part of the Tang dynasty's philosophical character.

Two foreign ideologies which, perhaps owing to their more substantial structure and establishment, made a more lasting impression were Judaism and Islam. Both were introduced to China at around the time of the founding of the Tang dynasty, again through contacts along the ancient Silk Road. Judaism survived in isolated communities until the nineteenth century and Islam, largely because it either was or became the religion of so many of China's border peoples and national minorities in the north and west, grew steadily, embracing many millions and surviving strongly to the present day.

Such foreign religions and faiths added flavour to an already rich philosophical tradition, and never more so than during the Tang dynasty, but they did not significantly affect the mainstream of Chinese thought. Their existence in China is a reflection of the character of the time.

After the establishment of the Buddhist faith in China during the preceding centuries of disunion, the Tang dynasty witnessed the flourishing of that religion. In broad terms, in the Tang dynasty Buddhism assumed a more Chinese character and became even more closely identified with the administration. It also responded to the more liberal and expressive attitudes and demands of the Tang people.

Philosophical debate that delved into the Indian origins of Buddhism had given rise to variant schools of the faith but it was not until the Tang that, firstly, the conditions for diverse schools to develop existed and, secondly, the Chinese penchant for categorization and classification finally identified those varying schools as sects. The number of Buddhist sects in Tang China reflects yet again the richness in thought and attitude on the one hand and, on the other, the desire for more subjective pageantry and imagery in religious activity and thought, as opposed to strict and hierarchical dogma.

In such an atmosphere it was the so-called *Paradise Sutras* that became the foundation of Buddhist doctrine in the Tang. The obvious appeal of an assured after-life in Paradise ensured the popularity of the *Jingtu* or Pure Land sect. *The Pure Land Sutra* embodied the basic Mahayana philosophy of salvation through faith and good conduct. Rebirth in the Western Paradise of Amitabha Buddha was assured to those who, in one version of the *sutra*, led lives full of meritorious deeds, or in the other version of the *sutra*, devoted their lives to faith and prayer. With the well-founded and widespread establishment of Buddhism, favoured and supported by the imperial court and reaching a broad spectrum of the populace through the popular imagery and pageantry of the basic Pure Land sect, the foundations for

Islam flourishes in parts of China to this day, particularly in the north-western border regions and along the routes of the ancient Silk Road. The Imam of Kucha, an ancient city lying on the northern route of the Silk Road midway between Turfan to the east and Kashgar to the west, is proud testimony to the strength of the faith, which was introduced into China in the Tang dynasty.

imaginative diversity in Buddhist thought were laid. Certainly the flowering of such sects is a feature of Buddhism in the Tang. The principal offshoot sects of Tang Buddhism were the *Zhenyan* (True Word), *Tiantai* (named after Mount Tiantai in Zhejiang province where the school was established), *Faxiang* (Characteristics of the Dharmas) and finally, the most enduring and influential, the *Chan* school of meditative Buddhism. In their own ways each of these, and indeed offshoot schools of lesser significance, fulfilled a philosophical and religious need in a progressive and enquiring Chinese population. But they did not enjoy the widespread acceptance of the more established Pure Land sect, and thus tended to find their followers among the educated classes.

The *Zhenyan* style of Buddhism, which appeared as an identifiable sect in the eighth century, was a form of esoteric Buddhism deeply influenced by Tantrism. The Sanskrit word *tantra* means 'that which spreads knowledge'. Tantric Buddhism had emerged in India where it had been much influenced by ancient Hindu mythologies and thus, among Buddhist purists, was thought to be a somewhat debased form of Buddhism. Within the Chinese sphere of influence it was subsequently to gain a dominant foothold in Tibet. Central to Tantric theory is the belief that Man is steeped in ignorance but that he can be released from that depressed state by discovering his 'divine spark', or Buddha-nature, through esoteric devotion and ritual. The world of Tantric Buddhism is a cosmos full of exotic gods and deities who are symbols of functions, energy and will. Magic and symbolism became the public façade of Tantrism and such themes were expressed in schematic cosmological and symbolical drawings and paintings known as

RIGHT *The interior of the Wanfo or Thousand Buddha cave that was carved in 680 at the Longmen cave temples near Loyang. The principal image is the 4m (13ft) high Amitabha Buddha, who is flanked by the monks Ananda and Kasyapa, Bodhisattvas and guardians. The ceiling is dominated by a lotus flower, around which is inscribed a dedication stating that the cave was commissioned by the eunuch Yao Shenbiao and the monk Zhi Yun in the first year of the Yonglong era of Emperor Gao Zong's reign. The cave takes its name from the estimated 15,000 miniature Buddha images carved into its northern and southern walls.*

BELOW *The entrance to the Wanfo cave showing the exterior cliff face covered with detailed carvings of Buddha, deities and guardian figures.*

mandalas, which were to become an influential component of Buddhist art in Japan. The use of symbolism and the emphasis on ceremonial in Tantric forms of Buddhism found a ready appreciation among a Chinese people to whom such ideas were already familiar through traditional Taoist and Confucian beliefs.

The *Faxiang* sect remained closer to the ideals of its Indian origin in its fundamental belief that the visible tangible world was nothing more than a fabrication of human consciousness, and thus an illusion. This was hardly likely to find mass appeal in a society whose values and ideals had been determined by down-to-earth Confucian virtues. Nevertheless the *Faxiang* school, started by the great pilgrim Xuan Zang (of whom more later) had a least some following, reaching a peak in the mid-Tang. Without its founder and inspiration the school quickly disappeared, suggesting that it had not made any real impact upon the hearts and minds of the general populace.

The *Tiantai* sect practised a style of Buddhism that moderated between the studied ritual of the formal schools and the subjective approach of the *Chan* school. It was founded towards the end of the sixth century by Zhi Yi, who proclaimed that true reality was a combination of meditation, concentration, study, moral discipline and ritual. The sect was eclectic, and possibly it was just that quality that was appealing. By the later eighth century it was arguably the most popular form of Buddhism in China. The sect's moderation and classification appealed to the Confucian formalism so prevalent in the Chinese ethic, while its admission of more subjective and contemplative notions satisfied a philosophical-emotional demand. The popularity of the *Tiantai* sect helped to establish the *Lotus Sutra* (which sought to reveal the true Buddha in the form of Sakyamuni who appeared on Earth to save all mankind) as the most widespread gospel of Buddhism in East Asia.

Of all the schools of Buddhism which had surfaced in Tang China it was ultimately the *Chan* sect which proved the most significant, largely through its substantial infiltration into the thought and style of first Chinese and subsequently Japanese life. To this day the concept of *chan* carries with it a universal appeal and a beguiling otherworldliness.

The basic theme of *Chan* Buddhism is that ultimate truth can be sought only through looking within. The *dhyani* exercise was the means to attain realization, or enlightenment. The *dhyani*, or *chan*, is the religious, intellectual and emotional discipline that tranquillizes the mind to a state in which the devotee can concentrate only on consciousness. Through meditation, an awareness of that faculty which transcends the finite world is achieved, and thus spiritual serenity.

Such notions struck a receptive chord in the minds of a people alert and sympathetic to Taoist values. Romantic, anti-establishment ideals of rustic simplicity, anti-scholarship, anti-clerical structure and self-reliance were seen as virtually a refreshed form of native Taoism. In combining with the imaginative and liberal attitudes of Taoism, *Chan* Buddhism thus became a major stimulus to the creative processes of art and literature in Tang China, and indeed in later eras. The absence of structure, ritual and establishment, and the emphasis upon simple self-sufficiency and contemplation were the real strengths of the school, and these gave *Chan* thought and philosophy the means to become absorbed into the ethic of Chinese society and, furthermore, to adapt to changing circumstances. After the Tang dynasty, *Chan* was the only form of Buddhism in China to continue to develop in an aura of vigorous debate and attention.

The beginnings of *Chan* Buddhism are generally dated to the arrival in north China, in the third decade of the sixth century, of the semi-legendary figure Bodhidharma, whose teachings had fallen upon deaf ears in the traditionally Chinese-orientated south. However, it was not until the early Tang dynasty that *Chan* Buddhism became firmly established and even then considerable debate surrounded its controversial teachings. At this time the sect had the main body of its followers in north China, and its then leader, Shen Xiu (605–706) continued to proclaim the need for studious contemplation and meditation in the search for 'gradual enlightenment'. This view was challenged by Shen Hui (670–762) and Hui Neng (638–713) who proposed the concept of 'sudden enlightenment' which became identified with the so-called Southern School of *Chan*. The philosophical debates that surrounded the notions of 'gradual' or 'sudden' enlightenment characterize the intellectual vigour of Tang dynasty China. The means by which Hui Neng emerged as the patriarch of the sect are worthy of note in this context.

According to the standard version of the history of *Chan* Buddhism, written in the eleventh century, Hui Neng was one day selling firewood, when by chance he heard some people reciting the *Diamond Cutter* (an abbreviated version of the *Perfection of Wisdom Sutra*) and was sufficiently impressed to seek guidance and instruction from Hong Ren, the then Patriarch of *Chan* Buddhism. Hong Ren said to his new disciple that southerners did not possess the Buddha-nature and that therefore Hui Neng should abandon his quest. Hui replied that the true Buddha-nature transcended such things, an answer which impressed the Patriarch. When the time came for Hong Ren to choose his successor as patriarch he declared that the mantle would pass to whoever who could best embody the *Chan* philosophy in a poem. At that time Shen Xiu was considered the obvious choice. He wrote the following poem:

> The body is the tree of enlightenment,
> And the mind is like a bright mirror-stand,
> Always cleanse them diligently, and do not
> Let dust fall upon them.[2]

Within a few days another poem was placed next to Shen Xiu's, offered by the humble firewood-seller, Hui Neng:

> Enlightenment is not a tree to begin with,
> Nor is the mind a mirror-stand,
> Since originally there was nothing, whereon
> Would the dust fall?[3]

Hui Neng's prompt retort was recognized as true and the mantle of Patriarch of *Chan* Buddhism was passed to him. This was the final triumph of the Southern 'sudden enlightenment' School over the Northern 'gradual enlightenment' School, which subsequently passed into virtual oblivion. The notion of 'sudden enlightenment' and the parallel of spontaneous expression was to have a profound effect upon certain artistic traditions, painting, calligraphy and poetry in particular, in late Tang China and thereafter.

Although the great Buddhist persecutions of 841–5 decimated the traditional Buddhist establishment in China, since they were directed against formal institutions that had permeated government and the administration, *Chan* Buddhism survived and continued to flourish. With no formal structure, no hierarchy and no establishment, *Chan* was purely a means to personal awareness and contentment; it had no aspirations to influence government and was, therefore, no threat. In addition, as the school developed and embodied so much of Taoist philosophy, it came to be seen not as a foreign ideology but as very much a native tradition.

Having considered the identifiable forms and direction of thought and philosophy in the Tang dynasty, something of the flavour and style of the minds of the people may be gained from a brief review of the lives of certain individuals who were the main protagonists in various areas of Tang philosophy.

No one individual in Tang China better characterized traditional Confucianism and the purity of the Chinese ethic than the official Han Yu (786–824). Han was a great traditionalist and fervent upholder of Confucianism who eschewed and

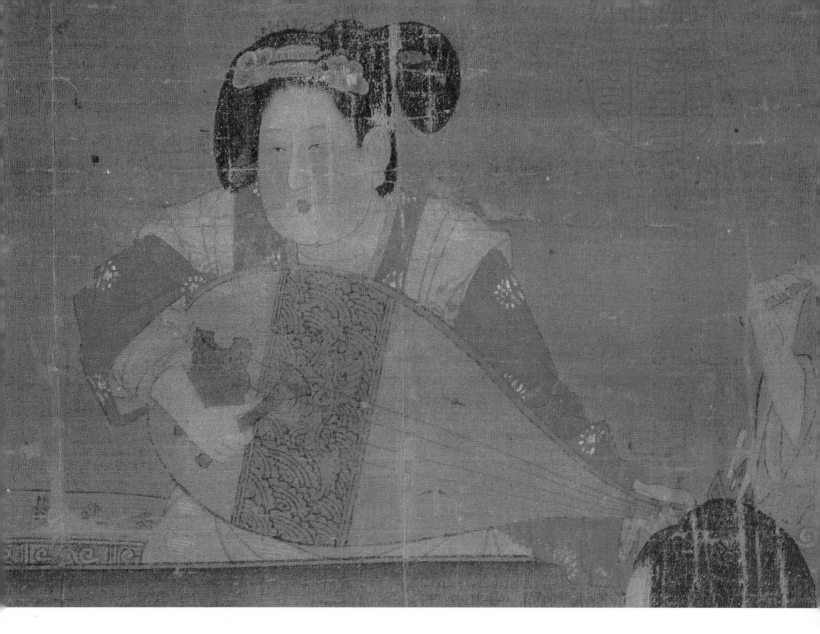

frequently opposed with determination the influences of foreign thought and ideals as debasing and irrelevant. After a career which, owing to his often out-spoken manner, was chequered, he rose to the position of Director of the Board of Rites. But he is best remembered for his contribution to prose literature and in this role his name is associated with the poets Li Bo and Du Fu as a member of the great literary trio of the Tang dynasty.

Han is famed, too, for one of his more outrageous deeds – the presentation of a memorial to the Emperor Xuan Zong, protesting against the proposed imperial acceptance of a bone of the Buddha. Brief excerpts from the lengthy submission indicate that Han was not given to reserved comment:

> Your servant begs leave to say that Buddhism is no more than a cult of the barbarian peoples which spread to China in the time of the later Han. It did not exist here in ancient times . . . . Now Buddha was a man of the barbarians who did not speak the language of China and wore clothes of a different fashion. His sayings did not concern the ways of our ancient kings, nor did his manner of dress conform to their laws. He understood neither the duties that bind sover-eign and subject, nor the affections of father and son. If he were still alive today and came to our court by order of his ruler, Your Majesty might condescend to receive him, but it would amount to no more than one audience in the Xuan Zheng Hall, a banquet by the Office for Receiving Guests, the presentation of a suit of clothes, and he would then be escorted to the borders of the nation, dismissed and not allowed to delude the masses . . . .[4]

An anonymous tenth-century painting of a palace concert illustrates the Tang style of figure painting and the style and flavour of Tang courtly life. Both paintings and tomb figures indicate that it was the task of the women of the court to perform as musicians, dancers and entertainers. The musician's patterned robes, hairstyle and made-up face reflect the fashions shown in the wall paintings of Tang tombs and pottery tomb figures.

Han Yu's passionate devotion to rekindling ancient ideals led to the birth of the Neo-Confucian movement which, as we have noted, had its roots in a form of cultural nationalism. However, his uncompromising attitude eventually led to his dismissal from officialdom to Chaozhou in present-day Guangdong province. There Han set himself the task of civilizing 'the rude inhabitants of those wild parts'. He even issued a denunciatory ultimatum to a huge crocodile that was causing distress and damage to the inhabitants. This ultimatum has become one of the almost legendary masterpieces of Tang prose and is worthy of full report:

On the twenty-fourth day of the fourth month of the fourteenth year of Yuanhe, Han Yu, Governor of Chaozhou, had his officer Chin Ji take a sheep and a pig and throw them into the deep waters of Wu creek as food for the crocodile. He then addressed it as follows:

When in ancient times the former kings possessed the land, they set fire to the mountains and the swamp, and with nets, ropes, fish-spears and knives expelled the reptiles and snakes and evil creatures that did harm to the people, and drove them beyond the four seas. When there came later kings of lesser power who could not hold so wide an empire, even the land between the Jiang and the Han they wholly abandoned and gave up to the Man and the Yi, to Qu and to Yue, let alone Chao which lies between the five peaks and the sea, some ten thousand li from the capital. Here it was that the crocodiles lurked and bred, and it was truly their rightful place. But now a Son of Heaven has succeeded to the throne of Tang, who is godlike in his wisdom, merciful in peace and fierce in war. All between the four seas and within the six directions is his to hold and to care for, still more the land trod by the footsteps of Yu and near to Yangzhou, administered by governors and prefects, whose soil pays tribute and taxes to supply the sacrifices to Heaven and Earth, to the ancestral altars and to all the deities. The

crocodiles and the governor cannot together share this ground. The governor has received the command of the Son of Heaven to protect this ground and take charge of its people; but you, crocodile, goggle-eyed, are not content with the deep waters of the creek, but seize your advantage to devour the people and their stock, the bears and boars, stags and deer, to fatten your body and multiply your sons and grandsons. You join issue with the governor and contend with him for the mastery. The governor, though weak and feeble, will not endure to bow his head and humble his heart before a crocodile, nor will he look on timorously and be put to shame before his officers and his people by leading unworthily a borrowed existence in this place. But having received the command of the Son of Heaven to come here as an officer, he cannot but dispute with you, crocodile: and if you have understanding, do you hearken to the governor's words.

To the south of the province of Chao lies the great sea, and in it there is room for creatures as large as the whale or roc, as small as the shrimp or crab, all to find homes in which to live and feed. Crocodile, if you set out in the morning, by the evening you would be there. Now, crocodile, I will make an agreement with you. Within full three days, you will take your ugly brood and remove southwards to the sea, and so give way before the appointed officer of the Son of Heaven. If within three days you cannot, I will go to five days; if within five days you cannot, I will go to seven. If within seven days you cannot, this shall mean either that finally you have refused to remove, and that though I be governor you will not hear and obey my words; or else that you are stupid and without intellect, and that even when a governor speaks you do not hear and understand.

Now those who defy the appointed officers of the Son of Heaven, who do not listen to their words and refuse to make way before them, who from stupidity and lack of intellect do harm to the people and to other creatures, all shall be put to death. The governor will then choose skilful officers and men, who shall take strong bows and poisoned arrows and conclude matters with you, crocodile, nor stop until they have slain you utterly. Do not leave repentance until too late.[5]

The final word on Han Yu belongs to the *New History of the Tang Dynasty*, for his most significant role in determining a new direction in Chinese philosophy that from the late Tang onwards rejected the notion of foreign ideals:

... Han Yu, though separated from Confucius by more than a thousand years, rejected the two schools of Taoism and Buddhism. In his destroying of confusion and restoring of orthodoxy, he equals Mencius in merit and doubles him in energy.[6]

The poet Du Fu (712–70) was as ardent as Han in his belief in the ultimate truth and destiny of Confucianism. He displayed the same kind of dogmatic attitude, even though he is acknowledged as a great poet in the greatest era of Chinese poetry. He was not, it seems, unaware of his ability and once even declared that he prescribed reading his poetry as a cure for malarial fever.

As a great Confucianist, and in keeping with the style and commitment of that philosophy, Du Fu's poetry displays little humour; restraint, pain and suffering emerge as virtues and reflect his grave Confucian moralist character. A conscientious upholding of the past is a consistent quality of his poetry, which invariably evokes a kind of classic heroism and noble endeavour:

> The jade palace is a void in the deserted temple.
> In the pines of the ancient shrine aquatic cranes nest;
> At summer and winter festivals the comers are village elders.
> The Martial Marquis's memorial shrine is ever nearby;
> In union, sovereign and minister share the sacrifices together.[7]

These words express melancholy at the passing of grandeur – jade palaces are isolated and only aquatic cranes occupy the ancient shrine.

Regarded as being as great a poet as Du Fu, but of a character and philosophy the very antithesis of Du's Confucian sombreness, was Li Bo (*c.* 705–62). Born into a distinguished family, he was recognized as a poet at the early age of ten. A traditional career in the rarefied intellectual world of officialdom was evidently at hand; however, Li Bo abandoned such conventions to roam the country in a romantic swashbuckling manner, devoting his time and energies to the two things indelibly linked with him, wine and poetry. With five colleagues of similar inclinations, he settled for some time in the mountains of, it is thought, Shandong province, where the group was known as the 'Six Idlers of the Bamboo Brook'. Such wistful, indulgent and affectionate terminology speaks for the esteem in which philosophers, poets and intellectuals were held in Tang China.

After his eventual arrival in Changan in around 742, Li Bo became the favoured poet of the Emperor Xuan Zong, and he contributed much to that court's atmosphere, which is renowned in the history of China for its lively cultural and artistic style. On one occasion, when summoned by the Emperor, the poet was finally found lying drunk in a street. Rescued and freshened with cold water he was made ready for the imperial presence and, with a lady attendant holding an ink slab, Li is reported to have dashed off impassioned lines of verse. These so impressed the Emperor that he instructed his most powerful eunuch to show deference by removing the poet's boots – a task which, not surprisingly, the eunuch considered a gross insult. The upshot was that the offended eunuch persuaded the Emperor's infamous consort, Yang Guifei, to intervene and have Li banished from the court. Li Bo, along with his colleagues, departed the imperial court and formed a coterie

The Cang Ling Ting or Surging Wave Pavilion garden in Suzhou, where scholars, poets and philosophers sought to encapsulate the grandeur of nature. The Chinese garden, a place of contemplation, classic elegance and studied ease, is one of the most extraordinary and distinctive of man-made environments with its contrived form of free expression, continuous flow and unexpected twists and turns. Its history reaching back to the Qin and Han dynasties, the Chinese garden had achieved maturity by the Tang and it was indeed the style of Tang gardens that influenced the development of the classic Japanese garden.

which went under the colourful name of the 'Eight Immortals of the Winecup'; they continued to frequent, and probably torment, the taverns and inns of Changan. According to popular legend, Li Bo drowned when, leaning from a boat, he tried to embrace a reflection of the moon.

Li Bo's philosophy was based on his belief in the spontaneous reaction to the rhythms and beauties of nature. Li represented an extreme version of the Taoist ideal, as he threw himself on the mercy of nature and life. The Taoist abandonment of Li Bo is captured in a brief verse:

> I sat drinking and did not notice the dusk,
> Till falling petals filled the folds of my dress.
> Drunken I rose and walked to the moonlit stream;
> The birds were gone, and men also few.[8]

The solitary communion with nature by means of which the Taoists sought ultimate insight into the Way was a strong element pervading Li's poetry, despite his obvious capacity for more gregarious conduct. This contemplative attitude, which also surfaced in the *Chan* Buddhist doctrine, and then flowed on into prose literature, painting and calligraphy, formed an important part of the intellectual character of the Tang dynasty. The theme of Man's harmony with nature is reflected in Li Bo's poem, 'On Hearing Jun [a monk] Playing the Lute':

> A monk from Shu, clasping a Luqi lute,
> Descends the west face of Omei peak.
> He sweeps his hand over the strings for me
> And I seem to hear pines sigh in a thousand ravines,
> And a running stream that washes the ache from my heart.
> The faint notes blend with the icy bells. [CONTD]

I had not noticed the dusk on the green mountains.
How many folds are hidden in the autumn clouds?[9]

A similar sensibility is illustrated in the works of another of the Tang dynasty's most illustrious poets, Wang Wei (699–759). Wang Wei was launched on a predictable official career having passed the *jinshi* examination in 721 and having subsequently been appointed an Assistant Minister at the Emperor Xuan Zong's court. He was at this time already famous as a poet, and when the An Lushan rebellion dislodged the Emperor, Wang Wei was removed to Loyang in order that the rebel general might 'see what sort of an animal a poet was!'. After such turbulence Wang Wei retired to the country to seek the solace and quietude of a scholar's life – the epitome of the intellectual ideal in Tang Society. Amid the mountains, Wang Wei put into verse essentially the same philosophy as the wayward Li Bo: a recognition of the harmony between Man and nature. A devout Buddhist, Wang expresses in his poetry the essential truth of the subjective, and in the classic mode of the scholar, seeks to shed the potentially impeding paraphernalia of life and society:

In evening years given to quietude,
The world's worries no concern of mine,
For my own needs making no other plan
Than to unlearn, return to long-loved woods:
I loosen my robe before the breeze from pines,
My lute celebrates moonlight on mountain pass.
You ask what laws rule 'failure' or 'success' –
Songs of fisherman float to the still shore.[10]

While a devotion to native philosophic traditions and values is a constant factor in the Tang, it was still the single most outward-looking period in the history of China. It would, therefore, be appropriate to conclude this chapter with a short description of a pilgrim who travelled far beyond the borders of the extensive Tang empire in search of inspiration and religious truth.

Perhaps the most famous Buddhist priest of Tang China, Chan Yi (602–64), known to posterity by his religious name of Xuan Zang, set out from Changan in 629 for India. His purpose was to visit the source of his adopted faith and seek further knowledge and understanding. He retured to China some seventeen years later, having journeyed across the desert wastes and bleak awe-inspiring mountain ranges of Central Asia into India, bearing over 650 major Buddhist texts, pictorial images and icons. He was received with great honour by the Emperor Tai Zong in 645, and rewarded with the title *San Zang* (Three Treasure Houses).

One of Xuan Zang's principal legacies was the record of his travels, the *Xiyu Ji*, which carries colourful and graphic descriptions of the distant and unfamiliar places through which he travelled: Turfan, Bactria, the Hindu Kush, Iran, Afghanistan and eventually India. When he finally arrived in India, Xuan Zang was struck by the contrast between the robust Afghans and the delicately-featured Hindus, whom he clearly did not admire, describing them thus:

By habit the people of the country live in luxury and happiness. They also like to sing. By nature, however, they are effeminate, soft, ill-tempered and treacherous. They treat each other with deceit and scorn and they never give way to another. They are small in stature and their movements are light and impetuous.[11]

Another version of Xuan Zang's travels, written in novel form and entitled *Record of a Journey to the West*, also translated in popular form as *Monkey*, describes the exploits of an all-competent monkey that accompanied the priest on his journey to the Western Paradise.

A Tang dynasty three-colour or sancai *glazed pottery model of a monkey holding a wine flask. The monkey is the ninth of the twelve animals corresponding to the twelve terrestrial branches but was also regarded in China as an emblem of ugliness and trickery. However, the monkey also became a virtual god, known as Sun Houzi, in popular Buddhism as hero and protector in the dramatized account of the monk Xuan Zang's travels known as the* Record of a Journey to the West.

After his return to the Middle Kingdom, Xuan Zang declined the constant exhortations of the Emperor to abandon monastic life in order to serve the imperial government as a political adviser, and dedicated his life to working on the material that he had acquired. In all he translated seventy-three of the hundreds of texts he had brought back, thereby adding a great new wealth of accessible material to the literature of Buddhism in China. Within the liturgy of the Buddhist faith his particular contribution was the introduction of the *Faxiang* school. However, his impact upon thought and philosophy must be seen in more general terms as offering new insights, styles, information and ideals from distant cultures. In that respect, Xuan Zang perhaps characterizes more than any other individual the real spirit of thought and attitude in Tang dynasty China.

5
CUSTOMS AND RITUAL
The Imperial Court
at Changan

The great Tang poet Bo Zhuyi (772–846) described the capital city of the mighty Tang empire in a single line: 'In Changan, the place of profit and fame.' The most cosmopolitan and colourful metropolis of its day, Changan inspired both poets and prose-writers. One of the most vivid descriptions is by the Arab traveller Ibn Wahhab, who arrived in China around 815 by the sea route. Having arrived at 'Kanfu' (the then port of Hangzhou) he travelled to Changan where, after presenting several petitions, he was finally lodged in a house upon imperial orders and subsequently granted an audience with the Emperor. This extract is taken from a twelfth-century Arabic manuscript entitled *Achbar ul Sin wal Hind* (*Observations on China and India*), which relates the stories of two ninth-century Arab travellers who visited China:

> We asked Ibn Wahhab many questions concerning the city of Cumdan (Changan), where the Emperor keeps his Court. He told us that the city was very large, and extremely populous; that it was divided into two great parts, by a very long and very broad street; that the Emperor, his chief ministers, the soldiers, the Supreme Judge, the eunuchs, and all belonging to the imperial household, lived in that part of the city which is on the right hand eastward; that the people had no manner of communication with them; and that they were not admitted into places watered by canals from different rivers, whose borders were planted with trees, and adorned with magnificent dwellings. The part on the left hand westward is inhabited by the people and the merchants, where are also great squares, and markets for all the necessaries of life. At break of day you see the Officers of the King's Household, with the inferior servants, the purveyors, and the domestics of the grandees of the Court, who come, some on foot, others on horseback, into that division of the city, where are the public markets, and the habitations of the merchants; where they buy whatever they want, and return not again to the same place till the next day.[1]

Contemporary Chinese descriptions of Changan convey quite a different flavour. No awe-inspiring details, wide-eyed panoramas, but poetic eulogies to the city's unrivalled role as the very epicentre of civilization. Li Bo captures the spirit of Changan in a poem he wrote when he was leaving the city for a distant provincial appointment:

Elements of the Tang architectural style that would have dominated the imperial buildings of Changan (present-day Xian) are well exemplified today in Japan. The Todaiji Temple in Nara boasts a number of buildings that reflect their Chinese origins, in particular the Nandaimon or 'Great South Gate'. The complex bracketing scheme to its interior is a traditional form of construction that did not require any extra support or even any rivets, nails or screws.

Long ago, among the flowers and the willows,
We sat drinking together at Changan.
The Five Barons and Seven Grandees were of our company.
But when some wild stork was afoot
It was we who fed it, yet boisterous though we were
In the arts and graces of life we could hold our own
With every dandy in the town –
In the days when there was youth in your cheeks
And I was still not old.
We galloped to the brothels, cracking our gilded whips,
We sent in our writings to the Palace of the Unicorn,
Girls sang to us and danced hour by hour on tortoiseshell mats . . . .[2]

The city's role as capital of the great centralized Chinese empire is echoed in the order and planning of Changan. Based on the grid pattern, the city's layout was determined by nine principal north-south and twelve east-west thoroughfares, all of which were contained within the rectangular plan of the overall city walls,

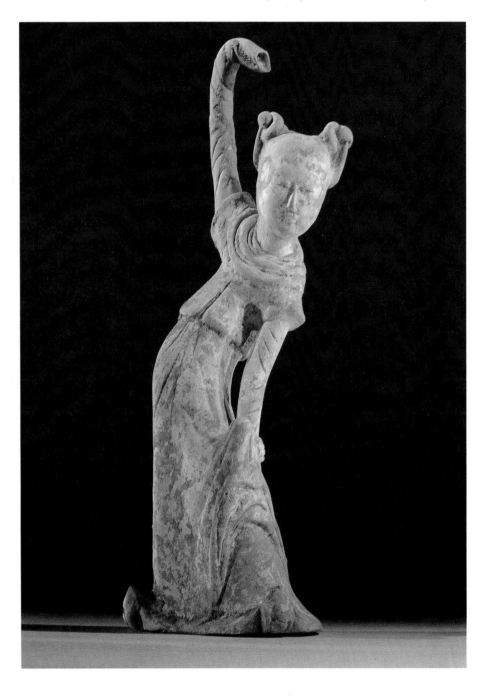

LEFT *An unglazed pottery tomb figure of a dancing lady distinguished by her twin topknot hairstyle and the long sleeves of her gown. It was the custom for female dancers at the Tang court to wear such distinctive costume, the long sleeves becoming an essential part of the energetic swirling dances that probably had their origin in Central Asia.*

RIGHT *Many of the most popular stage and theatrical dances of today are derived from the dances inspired by Western Asia that were the height of fashion in the Tang dynasty. In the north-western regions of China the music and dancing of Silk Road times is still to be seen and heard. Here a girl in Turfan pursues the 1400-year-old tradition that is a genuine echo of an ancient courtly pastime.*

covering an area of some thirty square miles (eighty square kilometres). The imperial enclave, in which were located the administrative offices of government and the secluded residential courtyards of the imperial palace, was situated in the centre of the northern sector.

Other major features of the city were the eastern and western markets where the cosmopolitan flavour of the metropolis could be savoured. In the area of the western market were concentrated the inns, tea-houses and business-houses of the foreign merchants from Central and Western Asia, India and beyond. Roman and Arabic coins of the period have been excavated in this district along with tombs of such Western visitors. It was within this area of the city that most of the foreign residents lived. According to records, which vary greatly, some four thousand families, from Central and Western Asia and as far afield as Persia and Iraq, were living in Changan in the late eighth century. This western section was undoubtedly the noisier, more exotic and vulgar part of town. In contrast, the eastern section and the eastern market were largely the preserve of the native Chinese population. Frequented as it was by the nobles and officials of the Tang hierarchy, a more restrained atmosphere prevailed here.

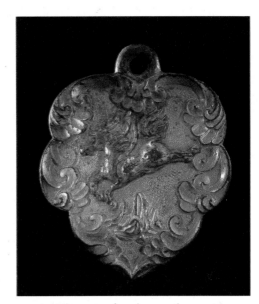

ABOVE *The sense of opulence and gregarious aesthetic expression that so characterized the spirit of the Tang court filtered down to the merest detail. Here a humble harness fitting of silvered and gilded bronze expresses that style with its flying mythical* qilin *and ornamental floral motifs.*

ABOVE *An unglazed and painted pottery model of a curly-headed and bejewelled youth probably from Western Central Asia – an evocative reminder of the Tang taste for the truly exotic.*

OPPOSITE *Introduced to China from Persia by way of the Silk Road, polo became a favoured sport with the Tang court. While pottery tomb models such as this dramatic and beautiful example glazed in green, cream and amber are comparatively rare, wall paintings in the tombs of members of the royal family such as Prince Zhang Huai illustrating polo playing are testimony to its popularity.*

To the visitor, it was the physical presence of Changan which was impressive: the city walls, watchtowers, gateways and gilded palaces, all on a grand scale and teeming with people. To the local populace it was the quality of life, the range of cultural qualities, the myriad experiences of such a cosmopolitan atmosphere and the mysterious aura that seats of great power exude which captured the imagination.

The sheer size of the city – thought to have been the largest in the world at that time, with a population of nearly two million – was perhaps the greatest source of wonder to the visitor. Of those two million people, it is thought that at least half lived within the city walls. Within those walls the central axis was described by Ibn Wahhab as that 'very long and very broad street', which ran from the south gate directly north to the very doors of the imperial city and from there to the palace. The records tell us that this impressive thoroughfare was no less than 152 metres (500 feet) in width. The two principal sections of the city divided by this axial route were further divided into rectangular blocks, which were in themselves administrative units within their own walls. No doubt certain individual characteristics and styles tended to emerge within such units. Such a rectangular plan of essential simplicity, effectiveness and logic formed the basis for the layout of the then capital of Japan, Nara (near present-day Kyoto), at the beginning of the eighth century. The essential order, overlain with concentration and bustle, is captured in this brief poem by Bo Zhuyi:

> Hundreds of houses, thousands of houses – like a great chess-board.
> The twelve streets like a huge field planted with rows of cabbages.
> In the distance I see faint and small the torches of riders to Court,
> Like a single row of stars lying to the west of the Five Gates.[3]

To the north-east of the imperial palace was another imperial enclave in which was situated the Daming (Great Brightness) Palace, built by Tai Zong, the second emperor. This was destined to become the centre of political power in Tang dynasty China. The Daming complex was within a very much larger rectangular area, the Imperial Park, where the emperor and members of the imperial family could enjoy some peace and their favoured pursuits: hunting, riding, archery and perhaps even polo.

The overall size of the walled Tang capital was very much larger than the city of today. Of the buildings constructed in the Tang dynasty, the two principal surviving edifices are the Dayan (Great Goose) Pagoda and the Xiaoyan (Little Goose) Pagoda, built in 652 and 707 respectively.

The evidence for the style and procedure of life at the Tang court is fragmentary and based on both literary and archaeological material. Once again, the records and memoirs of visitors and embassies from abroad provide evocative and colourful impressions. From an amalgam of such sources it seems that the procedures for an audience with the emperor of China were as follows. First, the visiting embassy would be lodged at a hostel on the very periphery of the city, at one of the main gates, for a few days. During that sojourn contact would be made with the Honglu office, an instrument of government which also served as a kind of foreign office. Meetings and discussions would follow in order that a brief, together with a map of the envoy's native land, might be prepared.

After such preliminaries, which may have taken weeks rather than days, the way was finally prepared for the imperial audience. Enormous care and attention to detail ensured that the envoy and his entourage would be impressed by the grandeur of the occasion and the imperial environment. Colourful ranks of officials, courtiers and guards were but a preamble to the awe-inspiring aloofness of the emperor himself, whose presence and solemnity were amplified by his total silence throughout the proceedings. According to the *Tang Shu* (*The Book of Tang*) the preliminary display of wealth and power would have included ranks of guards,

lancers, archers, swordsmen and halberdiers all with distinctive colours, banners and flags. Other troops, comprising the household guard, wore scarlet tunics and caps decorated with the tail feathers of the Manchurian snow pheasant or tabards of scarlet taffeta embroidered with wild horses. Upon reaching the imperial audience, after proceeding through the intimidating ranks of guards, the delegation would be required to prostrate themselves. The leader would then offer tribute, saying '. . . your loyal vassal of so-and-so nation presumes to present these offerings from our soil . . .'. The officer of protocol would accept the gifts on behalf of the still silent emperor.

In return, the visiting embassy would be presented with gifts, often bolts of silk which, oddly, were regarded as a 'salary', according to the Japanese monk Ennin. It was also customary for tribute-bearing envoys to be rewarded with a flattering and grand-sounding title which, in effect, was a tacit acknowledgement by the recipient of Chinese supremacy. Ennin records that the ambassador to the Japanese delegation was invested with such honorific titles as 'Cloud Banner General of China', 'Acting President of the Bureau of Imperial Sacrifices' and 'General of the Imperial Palace Guards of the Left'. When the King of Sribhoja, in far-off Sumatra, sent an envoy to the court of Xuan Zong, it is said that the Tang Emperor recognized the tribute by conferring on the distant king 'a robe of state and the title of Great Army Leader of the Militant Guards of the Left, and a purple caftan and a bolt inlaid with gold'.[4]

The temporary nature of the architecture of China, including that of the great cities such as Changan, with their buildings of timber and mud bricks, leaves us with a somewhat theatrical vision of life at the Tang court, as though the city was a backdrop of stage scenery which came and went, whereas the philosophy, the play, lived on. The settings of gilded palaces, ornately planned gardens, lakes and willow trees, are reflected in later Ming and Qing establishments that survive to this day. The imperial style of the Tang was very much the model for the dynasties that followed.

Similarly, Tang paintings or, as is more usual, copies of Tang paintings, convey an echo of that courtly style of life. Their fragmentary nature, combined with the inevitable Chinese tendency to formalize such representations, tends to heighten the impression of theatricality. One quality that is easily obscured with the passage of time is the sheer vibrancy of the colour that so enhanced the atmosphere. Surviving works of art do, however, retain much of this quality of the Tang dynasty's flavour and style – gold, silver, multi-glazed ceramics and richly woven silks reveal the taste for a highly decorative style and the delight in sophisticated technology.

RIGHT *The role of the courtly lady in the imperial palace is illustrated in an unglazed pottery model of an imposing and haughty figure holding an offering vessel. The graceful simplicity of the lines is a convincing testimony to the sophisticated style and aesthetic of the Tang court.*

ABOVE *A glazed pottery figure of a kneeling female musician holding a flute, with a distinctive high chignon hairstyle. This would have been one of a group of musicians representing a courtly ensemble that would have been placed in the tomb of a deceased member of the imperial family.*

In costume, too, where again foreign styles were so popular, the elegant, often complex hairstyles and the vogue for cosmetics reflect the richness of a cosmopolitan attitude. Yellow, blue, green, red and black powders were widely used as cosmetics by ladies at the Tang court to enhance their appearance. A purple powder used as mascara was, it is thought, imported from Persia. Such fanciful indulgences, like exotic jewellery, added glamour and colour to the court scene, but also provoked some hostility from traditionalists and mirth among the scholars and poets. Towards the end of the dynasty, almost certainly as a consequence of the anti-foreign movement, a more severe style of make-up and general appearance became fashionable.

After the ministers, aristocrats, officials, scholars and eunuchs, the most significant people of the court were the ladies. The officials and ministers whose business was the management of the empire were largely confined to ministry buildings and imperial audience halls in the conduct of their affairs. The so-called Inner Palace of the imperial compound was literally the Forbidden City – even the highest ministers of state were excluded from this area inhabited only by the emperor, his younger children before they established their own households, the harem, the eunuchs and a sizeable body of female attendants. There were, for example, no less than 122 ladies with official grades in the Inner Palace; ranging from the empress through the ranks of Noble, Pure, Virtuous and Good, which comprised the First Grade of lady at the court, to a series of ranks within grades which bore such evocative titles as 'Cultivated Beauty' and 'Accomplished One', to the lowest of all such ranks, described merely as 'handmaiden'.

Imperial ceremonial occasions ranged from impressive sacrificial rites to the relatively mundane audiences granted to foreign delegations and embassies. As the physical manifestations symbolizing the power and authority of the emperor, rites and ceremonies were considered to be of the greatest importance, and any failure to follow the prescribed formats would be interpreted as a sign of weakness and carelessness. Such things could prejudice the maintenance of the Mandate of Heaven.

Most important and awesome of the imperial rites were the *feng* and *shan* sacrifices, which were a symbolic statement to Heaven and Earth that the emperor had fulfilled his duties, that he had truly accepted and satisfied the requirements of the Mandate of Heaven. They were therefore an expression of extreme confidence. So weighty was the burden of commitment that the *feng* and *shan* sacrifices represented that they were very rarely performed. Should the emperor have been misled into believing that it was a propitious time for the sacrifices, Heaven would no doubt seek vengeance and the Mandate of Heaven would be threatened. The sacrifices were performed at China's most sacred mountain, Taishan, in Shandong province.

The first time during the Tang dynasty that they were performed was in AD 666, and they had been celebrated only six times before in recorded history, the last occasion having been in AD 56 – in the Han dynasty. They were performed only once more in the Tang, by Xuan Zong in 725. The description of Xuan Zong's entourage gives an idea of the scale of such undertakings. The retinue of attendants, officials, relatives, scholars and foreign leaders set out from the eastern capital, Loyang, and arrived at Taishan after a month on the road. The imperial convoy stretched 'for miles' and wherever they halted the many thousands of personnel literally laid waste the countryside. The return journey had to be by a different route simply because no village or town could have supported two such visits within a short space of time.

The purpose of these and other such rites and sacrifices was to maintain the harmony between Man and the determining forces of nature and the cosmos. To assure such harmony was, beyond doubt, the emperor's most vital role, as was clearly stated in the ancient *Record of Ritual (Li Ji)* which was compiled in late Zhou and early Han times:

The classic image of the Tang dynasty is illustrated in this glazed pottery tomb figure of a court lady holding a lotus stem. It was the usual practice to leave the faces of such figures unglazed in order to allow for the painting of facial features and details. Traces of the original pigments may be seen in the eyebrows, eyes, lips and cheek rouge on this figure.

When the former emperors presented their offerings to God in the outskirts of the capital, wind and rain were duly regulated, and cold and warmth came each in its appointed season, so that the Sage Emperor had only to stand with his face to the south for order to prevail throughout the world.[5]

Harmony between Heaven and Earth could only be maintained by Man participating in the cosmic patterns through appropriate ritual. That ritual could only be performed by the arbiter between Heaven and Earth, the Son of Heaven, the emperor.

Sacrifices were conducted on the summer and winter solstices and the most elaborate rites were performed to seek the concurrence of Heaven in the provision of a good harvest. One of the most enduring of the great imperial sacrifices was made, according to ancient ritual, '. . . at the winter solstice, a sacrifice to Heaven in the southern suburbs in order to greet the arrival of lengthening days'.[6] Such sacrifices, which implied a plea for a good harvest, continued at the Temple of Heaven in Beijing even into the post-dynastic era, the last being performed by President Yuan Shikai in 1915. Sacrifices to ancestors were also endlessly performed in accordance with Confucian tradition, showing continued respect for the past.

While particular sacrifices, such as the *feng, shan* and winter solstice offerings, were held at nominated sites, many of the imperial ceremonies were held within the confines of the palace. Such ceremonies would include diplomatic receptions, gatherings of officials and scholars to pay homage to the emperor, religious ceremonies involving Buddhist, Taoist and Confucian devotions, and the celebration of traditional seasonal festivals including the mid-autumn harvest festival, the New Year festival and the *qingming* spring festival. The gilded halls and palace buildings that reflected the style and aspirations of imperial Tang China have long since disappeared, but an impression is gained from the fifteenth-century Forbidden City of the Ming emperors in Beijing, built in a style going back to earlier Song, Tang and even Han times. Furthermore, literary records substantiate the grandiose schemes of the Tang court. One of the more accurate and telling descriptions provided by the Tang historians is of the Empress Wu's architectural monuments at her imperial seat, Loyang. The Ming Tang, 'Hall of Brightness', was built as the supreme expression of imperial architectural grandeur and consecrated to the supreme deity, Shang Di, literally 'Emperor Above'. There had been plans to build such a hall earlier in the dynasty, as it was thought such a building had existed centuries before in the Zhou dynasty; the intention was to recreate the image and

RIGHT *The drum tower at the Horyuji Temple in Nara in Japan is an eloquent echo of the Tang architectural style. In the late seventh and early eighth centuries, when the Horyuji Temple was founded, direct contacts between China and Japan and the frequent exchanges of embassies, priests and scholars brought to Japan the richness of Tang culture, from Buddhism to Sassanian-style silks to architecture.*

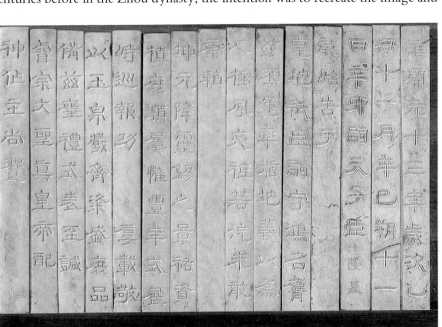

LEFT *Jade sacrificial tablets used by the Tang Emperor Xuan Zong when performing the vital* shan *sacrifices to the Earth in 725. The invocation inscribed on the jade tablet would have been read aloud by the Emperor during the ceremonies, in which he would reiterate his status as ruler and acknowledge his role as the recipient of the Mandate of Heaven. After the ceremonies the jade tablets were buried under the alter and it is recorded that these very tablets were subsequently re-excavated by the Song Emperor Tai Zong at the end of the tenth century, used in the* shan *sacrifices again and then re-buried, never apparently to be used or seen again until their discovery in 1928.*

One of the most beautiful and earliest surviving buildings in China is the Lower Huayan Monastery in the northern city of Datong. The graceful and imposing proportions, delicately sloping walls and wonderful sweeping rooflines are the perfect expression of the Tang architectural style even though these buildings were constructed a little over a century after the end of the Tang dynasty, in the early part of the eleventh century.

style of that bygone age. However, no records of that building could be found and the project lapsed until resurrected by the ever-ambitious Empress Wu.

Construction began in 688 within the palace compound under the supervision of the infamous cosmetic-pedlar confidant of the Empress, Xue Huaiyi, who by now was imperial architect. Thanks to the thousands of workers employed, the Ming Tang was completed in only a year, and is described in the *Tang Shu* (*The Book of Tang*) thus:

> There were three storeys, with a total height of [90 metres] 294 feet. The lowest, standing for the Four Seasons, had each of its four faces coloured to correspond to its orientation. The middle storey stood for the Twelve Branches [the Duodenary Cycle of symbols used to divide the twenty-four hours of the day into two-hour periods] and was crowned by a round cupola, supported by nine dragons. The top storey signified the Twenty-four Solar Periods of the year; it too had a round cupola. The whole was topped by a gilded iron phoenix, [three metres] ten feet high. Running up the middle, so as to connect bottom and top was a huge wooden pillar of ten span circumference.[7]

This massive timber pillar, which was probably the pivotal support of the whole structure, was not only functional; it almost certainly had a symbolic role representing the great axis between Heaven and Earth, the latter in the form of the imperial presence. A second hall, the Tian Tang, or 'Heavenly Hall', was built adjacent to the Ming Tang in the form of a five-storey pagoda to house a wooden figure of the Buddha so huge that 'several tens of men could stand on its little finger'. One of the more extraordinary ceremonies performed before this Great Buddha was that known as the 'Wu Zhe Hui' – the 'Unscreened Festival', one of those rare events to which the local populace was admitted, at which money was thrown into the crowd. In 695 this ceremony adopted an even more peculiar format with the digging of a pit fifteen metres (fifty feet) deep which was filled with images of the Buddha. These were then, by mechanical means, made to rise up before the astonished audience of peasants and locals. Then an ox was sacrificed and its blood smeared on the Buddha's head some sixty metres (two hundred feet) above ground level. Apparently the dreaded Xue Huaiyi became so carried away that he joined in, cutting his leg and smearing his own blood on the Buddha.

These buildings, which were in so many ways the physical manifestation of the notion of imperial grandeur, were not destined for a long career. As Xue Huaiyi began to lose his grip, he became violently jealous of those around him who were increasing their power and influence, and was subject to fits of incredible pique. In one he set fire to both the Ming Tang and the Tian Tang, reducing the great buildings to ashes. Both were rebuilt after Xue had been removed from the court and slain.

One problem facing any ruler or ambitious aristocrat or official in ancient China was the all-pervasive Confucian morality. Members of the imperial Tang court, like others before and after, undoubtedly indulged in awe-inspiring excesses, whether architectural, ceremonial, ritual or even to do with burial practices, but they were often pulled back from the brink of an overwhelming undertaking by the Confucian ethic of austerity. For example, the second emperor, Tai Zong, gained great popularity through ordering that his mountain palace be roofed with thatch rather than with more exotic coloured tiles. In 827 a government edict was issued commanding that officials desist from using extravagant and ostentatious architectural decorative features on their houses, such as hanging fish and phoenix-form roof tiles. Another decree of that same year listed the sizes of halls and gatehouses according to the rank of the official. Officials of the seventh rank and lower could build halls no larger than three bays across and two deep. Third rank officials could build halls up to a size of five bays by four. Only princes and above

The Nandaimon or 'Great South Gate' of the Todaiji Temple in Nara, Japan, is typically Tang Chinese in conception, but in its proportions reflects the three-bay square plan of the later Song dynasty which was adapted in an asymmetrical form by the Japanese Zen sects.

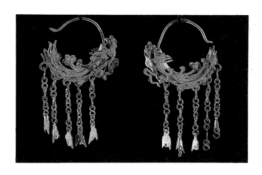

These silver earrings, encrusted in parts with malachite and shaped in the form of a mythical dragon-like creature, were probably once worn by a Tang dynasty empress or princess. The ends of the silver wire loops are sharpened to a point, suggesting that they were worn through pierced ears.

RIGHT *A stone mythical animal or* qilin *guarding the spirit road to the entrance of the tomb of the mother of Empress Wu near Qianling. The* qilin, *which resembles the Western unicorn, is one of the four great mythical animals of China, the others being the dragon, the phoenix and the tortoise. Distinguished by its abbreviated wings and stunted single horn, this fabulous creature of good fortune is also a traditional symbol of longevity, grandeur, felicity, illustrious offspring and wise administration.*

could have a two-storey gatehouse or use superimposed brackets and cupola ceilings. The Confucian sense of hierarchy and the social order which that hierarchy imposed was everywhere present in China.

Perhaps the most significant testimony to imperial vision is in the burial ground of the Tang royal family. The imperial tombs of the Tang court are located to the north of the present-day city of Xian, at Qianling and Zhaoling. The almost serried ranks of man-made hillocks, punctuated by the very much larger artificially shaped hills of the emperors' tombs, are an enticing reminder of the splendour of the Tang court, for many have still to be excavated to reveal the treasures they have concealed over the past twelve to thirteen centuries. The fact that the treasures which those few tombs already excavated have revealed were made exclusively for the tombs is an indication of the importance attached to burial ritual and ceremony. In seeking to reflect the earthly life of the deceased, such mausoleums have much to tell, too, of the life-style of the Tang courtiers. Their splendid and luxurious life on earth was not to be interrupted by death, so into the tomb went a wealth of material goods.

The structure of the Tang imperial tomb, like the associated ritual, was based on historical precedent. The chamber itself was excavated well below ground level and approached by a sloping roadway down which the cortège would be wheeled. The walls of the road were painted with scenes from the court of the deceased, and small niches cut into the wall contained pottery tomb figures representing officials, guardians, attendants, domestic and other animals who had been in the service of the dead person, and precious gold and silver items. Towards the bottom of the sloping roadway, where it levelled out before the final approach passage, was placed a memorial tablet with an appropriate epitaph. The passage then continued into the chamber itself, the walls again painted with scenes and figures closely

A distant view of the impressive artificially shaped hill marking the joint tomb of Emperor Gao Zong and Empress Wu at the Tang imperial burial grounds at Qianling near Xian. The tomb has yet to be excavated, although those of lesser royalty such as Prince Zhang Huai and Princess Yong Tai in the same grounds have been explored, with finds of many hundreds of tomb objects, treasures and wall paintings. What treasures this monumental tomb still conceals is probably beyond our estimation.

associated with the deceased, such as retainers bearing gifts or offerings. Finally it reached the chamber itself, in which was placed a stone sarcophagus in the form of a small building, carved or incised with figurative and symbolic images, with decorative features in the finest style. The size of the complex and the richness of the furnishings varied according to the rank and importance of the person buried there. Guardian figures, derived from the Four Heavenly Kings of Buddhism known as *lokopalas*, whose task it was to deter evil spirits from entering the tomb, were placed in each corner.

Outside, the tomb was marked by a pyramidal mound which, for lesser members of the Tang royal family, aristocrats and high-ranking ministers, was in the region of thirty metres (a hundred feet) in height; the tombs of emperors could be marked by a mountain shaped by Man that was more than 150 metres (500 feet) in height – like those of the Emperor Gao Zong and the Empress Wu at Qianling.

All such major tombs were approached by a 'spirit road', lined by huge stone carvings of animals, human figures and mythical beasts which guarded the tomb, leading to the entrance on the eastern side of the burial. The most famous of such imperial burial-ground approaches is that leading to the tombs of the Ming emperors in the northern outskirts of Beijing. In the case of satellite tombs the 'spirit road' was marked by a small number of selected stone figures, particularly lions, which again served to protect the entrance. A memorial tablet, or stele, was erected as a final announcement of the entrance to the tomb. Tombs of the emperors were approached by a 'spirit road' of far greater dimensions, these too lined with stone carvings of human and animal guardian figures.

These highly elaborate burials in Tang dynasty China were based on the philosophic premise that the end of life on Earth was not the end of life. The continuity of the dynasty was paramount and such impressive burials of the leaders of the dynasty played a vital role in lending substance to the notion of dynastic immortality.

6

BEYOND THE WHITE DRAGON DUNES
Foreign Contacts and the Taste for the Exotic

The erratic and wayward first son of the great Emperor Tai Zong, a neurotic maverick, took to living within the palace grounds in the imperial capital in a Turkish felt tent, attended by servants in Turkish sheepskin coats with their hair in pigtails, spoke only Turkish and fed himself on lumps of skewered mutton roasted over the camp-fire. Even in the gregarious and outward-looking Tang dynasty such conduct was considered to be less than seemly, particularly for a nominated crown prince, whose style and conduct was supposed to accord with the general demeanour of the court. The conspicuous pennant bearing the wolf's head emblem of the Turks that fluttered above the Prince's imperial camp was the final provocation.

Things foreign, whether the music and dances of the Tocharians, the gold and silver ewers of the Persians, the exotic fragrances of frankincense and myrrh from the Middle East or rugs from Turkestan, were the fashion of the day in Tang China. The response to the peoples of those distant lands was less enthusiastic, however, and any serious adoption of their life-styles, customs and habits rather than their products was greeted with cool aloofness.

The ultimate source of this taste for the exotic was trade. Overland and overseas trade reached unprecedented heights in the Tang dynasty and brought to the Middle Kingdom material and ideological visions which so broadened cultural horizons that the Tang dynasty is generally, and justly, acknowledged as a 'golden age' in the history of China. Merchandise supported this trade, but the real and enduring effect of commerce was not so much the availability of Western products in Chinese markets or of Chinese products in Western markets, but the social and cultural intercourse that resulted from it. This exchange gained depth and breadth as the trade routes between China and her mercantile partners crossed different countries and cultures.

Of all the great trade routes of the ancient world none has quite the mystique of the 'Silk Road'. That tenuous but tenacious thread between the capital of the Tang empire, Changan, and the cities of the Middle East – Samarkand, Palmyra, Antioch – and of the Eastern Mediterranean – Constantinople, Venice and Rome – bridged East and West across some of the most inhospitable regions known. The geography of that great 'in-between' would seem to suggest that nature had conspired to design a no-man's-land between the great cultures of the world. The arid heart of Central Asia is surrounded by high and awe-inspiring mountain ranges to the north, south and west, and by the Gobi desert in the east. The Taklamakan desert, stretching nearly 1600 kilometres (1000 miles) east to west and

True Silk Road territory – desert wastelands and bleak watchtowers near Dunhuang that in the Tang dynasty were manned by soldiers to ensure the safety of China's borderlands. As a result, Tang China benefited from a regular flow and interchange of ideas as well as merchandise.

500 kilometres (300 miles) north to south, was the wilderness which divided East from West. This desolate, deeply inhospitable and sparsely populated region became the meeting point between East and West and gave rise to an art and culture that flourished briefly, reaching its apogee during the Tang dynasty. The inspiration of Buddhism in this achievement was paramount, but it was an influence largely eclipsed in the tenth century with the advent of Islam in the region. With the passing of the Buddhist era, so too went the spiritual basis to the art and culture of Chinese Turkestan.

The foundations of this shortlived but inspired cultural phenomenon lay in trade and commerce along the ancient silk routes. On leaving the western gates of the Tang capital the camel trains of merchants would head north-west, and skirt the south-western border of the Gobi desert to reach the city of Lanzhou and from there the oasis town of Dunhuang. Here the traditional route divided in order to circumvent the dreaded Taklamakan desert, where the salt-encrusted wastelands inspired the description 'white dragon dunes'. In summer the temperature rises above 50°C (125°F) but in winter the ink froze in the pen of Sir Aurel Stein, the explorer-archaeologist whose expeditions at the beginning of this century helped to bring Central Asia and its fascinating ancient art to the attention of the Western world.

The rediscovery of Chinese Central Asia at the end of the nineteenth century and the early decades of the twentieth century by European, Russian and Japanese archaeologist-explorers was an event that caused widespread excitement. The idea of this distant wasteland re-emerging from the past, bringing forth artistic and

historical treasures of a great, distinctive, but generally extinct culture, revealing the secrets of ancient trade routes and hitherto unknown contacts between East and West, captured the public imagination. The competition between the archaeological protagonists of differing nations further fired public interest. When the very first formal report of Western expeditions was made to the 1899 International Congress of Orientalists in Rome, the German delegation's report contained the following:

> . . . a great stir was caused by the presentation of a magnificent collection of relics from the western part of Eastern Turkestan, in the possession of the British government, and by the report of the discoveries of a Russian expedition in the east of the same area. These finds and investigations brought home to us the astonishing fact that Eastern Turkestan possessed a rich and flourishing culture right up to the end of the first millennium, reflecting in its extraordinarily varied aspects the influence of the neighbouring Chinese, Indian and Greek–Western Asian cultures.

The British collection comprises manuscripts and woodcuts, coins and seals, terracottas and other figures, which were found in tombs, towers and other edifices, or dug up on sites buried in sand drifts.

The most important discovery of the Russian expedition (1898) was the finding of no less than 160 man–made cave complexes, being imitations of the world–famous Buddhist monastery and temple complexes of India, which often have subterranean elements. Many of these temples are adorned with Chinese, Indian and Turkish inscriptions, and above all with magnificent frescoes of religious and secular character.

BELOW *The upper section of a glazed pottery amphora with magnificent dragon-headed handles. Another example of the influence and inspiration of foreign styles on the art and attitude of Tang China, for the amphora shape echoes a similar Persian metal-work form.*

LEFT *The vast majority of the trade that the Silk Road sustained was handled not by the Chinese but by the nomadic peoples of Central and Western Asia. The Tang people generally reacted to them with amusement and interest, an attitude which is evident in the way they were depicted in art. Typical is this glazed pottery figure of a camel groom or trader with his exaggeratedly enormous nose.*

The great significance among the discoveries attaches to the manuscripts, most of which are in totally unknown scripts and tongues, presenting Orientalists overnight with a number of fascinating problems of the greatest import, the solution of which would constitute a great leap forward in the study of Central Asian scripts, languages and history . . . .[1]

The variety and richness of influences in the region were manifest, and evocatively illustrated by those manuscripts, which included examples of no less than seventeen different languages in twenty-four scripts.

The silk roads were more than just mercantile channels, for they became the well-trodden paths of monks, pilgrims, missionaries, diplomatic embassies, military expeditions and government officials. Here is the monk Xuan Zang's description of his first encounter with the forbidding Taklamakan desert:

There are no birds overhead, and no beasts below; there is neither water nor herb to be found . . . . At this time in the four directions, the view was boundless, there were no traces either of man or horse, and in the night the demons and goblins raised fire-lights as many as the stars; in the day-time the driving wind blew the sand before it as in the season of rain.[2]

The evocative ruins of the ancient Tang city of Gaochang, an outlying command and staging post on the Silk Road near Turfan. In the background is the so-called 'Flaming Mountain' which prevented the monk Xuan Zang from travelling further on his epic journey to India and the source of Buddhism in the seventh century until he had received the iron fan with which to quell the flames.

On the evidence of surviving Buddhist sites it seems that the northern route was the more popular, for the relics of monasteries, temples and pagodas along the foothills of the Tian Shan far outnumber those discovered along the southern route. However, numerous oasis sites along the southern route make it clear that its mercantile role was equivalent to that of the northern route.

It was along these routes that the trains of two-humped Bactrian camels, those sneering, cantankerous beasts of burden, endowed with an extraordinary resilience, carried their loads of merchandise. These ungainly animals not only survived but prospered, thanks to their ability to sniff out subterranean water and to predict the deadly sandstorms that afflicted the desert regions.

> When such a wind is about to arrive, only the old camels have advance knowledge of it, and they immediately stand snarling together, and bury their mouths in the sand. The men always take this as a sign, and they too immediately cover their noses and mouths by wrapping them in felt. This wind moves swiftly, and passes in a moment, and is gone, but if they did not so protect themselves they would be in danger of sudden death.[3]

These cunning camels managed to transport 200 kilograms (440 pounds) of cargo, silks from China and metal, glass, aromatics, perfumes and jewels from the Western world.

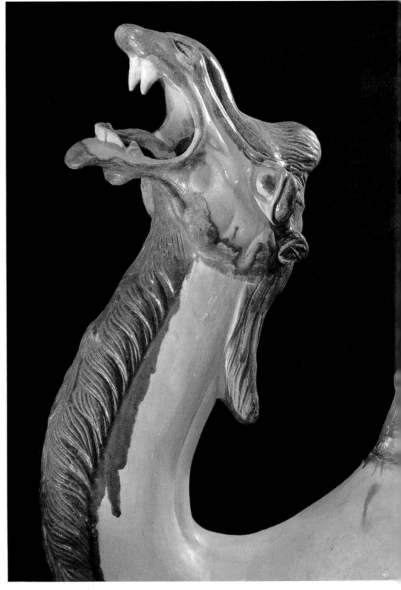

The fabled silk roads were, however, not the only routes that sustained international trade and cultural exchange during the Tang dynasty. Shipping routes from the Shandong peninsula linked China with Japan and Korea. In the eighth century, Japan opened up new sea routes between Nagasaki and the Yangzhou-Hangzhou regions. But the overseas trade routes of the greatest significance were those from the southern port of Canton, through the South China Sea, the Indian Ocean and on to the Persian Gulf. Ships laden with silks and ceramics would leave Canton in the late autumn or early winter, thus taking advantage of the monsoon winds to carry them across the Indian Ocean. At the same time Islamic ships were under sail, having left Basra or Siraf for South-East Asia and eventually Canton. Such trade was carried by ships manned principally by Persian crews, and Persian became the accepted language of the sea-borne trade between China and the Middle East. Ships sailing under the Chinese flag were a rarity, for it was not until later that the great era of ocean-going Chinese ships was to dawn.

Arab literature contains many references to 'Chinese ships' in the ports of the Persian Gulf in the seventh and eighth centuries, but such descriptions probably refer to vessels engaged in trade with China. Vessels from Ceylon, reputedly the largest of their kind, over 60 metres (200 feet) in length and carrying 600 to 700 men, were also active in the shipping business between the Middle East and China during the Tang period.

LEFT *The meeting of east and west in Canton (Guangzhou) at the Memorial Mosque to the Prophet, the Huai Sheng Si, more usually known as Beacon Tower Mosque, where the Islamic minaret rises above the roofline of traditional Chinese architecture. The mosque is reputedly the oldest in China and was built early in the Tang dynasty – when the port city was a thriving commercial centre with a cosmopolitan population second only to that of ancient Changan – by the Arab missionary Abu Waggas as a memorial to Mohammed.*

ABOVE *The art of Chinese Central Asia had a distinctive flavour in the Tang dynasty, drawing upon both local Central Asian and metropolitan Chinese styles, as is evident in this painted model of a soldier found in a tomb near Turfan.*

A most significant consequence of this commercial activity was the emergence of sizeable foreign communities in the principal trading cities of China, but the movements of foreigners, and particularly merchants, were severely limited, mainly to certain areas within those ports of entry. The distribution of goods from that point was in the hands of the Chinese. Commerce was a profession held in low esteem by the traditional Confucian hierarchy. Nevertheless the merchants thrived. It was a time when a traveller could '. . . visit Jing or Xiang in the south, Tai-yuan or Fanyang in the north, or Sichuan and Liangfu in the west, and everywhere there were shops and emporiums for supplying merchant travellers. Though they should go as far as several thousand *li* they need not carry even an inch-long blade.'[4]

The character of the great cities of the north, Changan and Loyang, was wildly cosmopolitan. Changan, in particular, with its population of Tocharians, Sodgians, Turks, Uighurs, Mongols, Arabs, Persians and Hindus, seemed to contain within its walls a world in microcosm. The poet Li He (791–817) wrote, 'Changan is a kingdom of jade and cassia'[5]; this was a wry comment on the cost of living in the city, for his implication was that food was dearer than jade, and firewood more costly than cassia (a type of cinnamon).

The colourful life around the inns and taverns of Changan and the 'godly' capital of Loyang, where Western girls served wine in amber and agate cups, and dancing girls and boy musicians from distant lands entertained in order to maintain the ardour and the tempo of sales, has been described by the writers of the Tang. Li

The tomb of Abu Waqqas in Canton, close to the mosque which he founded. The commercial foundations of Canton and the foreign populations which that trade supported have left an indelible mark on the character of the city, which today maintains a more cosmopolitan flavour than most Chinese cities. Indeed Canton still retains a sizeable Islamic population.

Bo evokes 'a Western houri beckoning with her white hand, inviting the stranger to intoxicate himself with a gold beaker of wine'.[6]

The ship-borne trade to the south stimulated the growth of a different kind of foreign community. Canton, then regarded as something of a frontier town plagued with wild beasts, unpleasant diseases and an uncomfortable climate, became an important commercial centre in the Tang dynasty with a population in excess of a quarter of a million. The Buddhist priest Jian Zhen, who travelled to Canton in 748, wrote lyrically of 'the argosies of the Brahmans, the Persians and the Malays, their number beyond reckoning, all laden with aromatics, drugs and rare and precious things, their cargoes heaped like hills'.[7]

Much of the trade that entered China through the port of Canton found its way to the more populous and prosperous north via Yangzhou, itself a port at the beginning of the Grand Canal system – the so-called 'River of Transport'. This city, too, expanded rapidly in the healthy economic climate of Tang China to become an important mercantile city through its general trade and distribution services, its role as the centre of the salt monopoly and as a banking centre and gold market. Yangzhou was the focus of trade with Japan and inevitably attracted foreign merchants, particularly Arabs involved in the sea-borne trade.

Commercial activity with both neighbouring and more distant countries brought with it an awareness of foreign ideals and fashions that rapidly developed into a tangible demand for specific goods and services. Apart from the obvious spoils of military expansion, particularly in Central Asia, and the consequent capture of hordes of Mongols, Manchus, Koreans, Tibetans, Uighurs and Sodgians, such peoples were also brought to the capital and major cities to serve as horseherds, grooms and camel attendants, and slaves. The new Tang territories in the south introduced a vogue for peoples of Indian and South-East Asian origin, the 'wavy-haired' people called 'Kurung' and 'Zangi', general terms for dark-skinned people who often had a penchant for relative nudity, much to the disgust and fascination of the prudish Chinese court.

The sylph-like beauties of Cambodia and Thailand were much favoured as dancing-girls or attendants in the courts of Changan and Loyang, and the taste for the 'Western' music and dances of Indian inspiration that were so popular among the nomadic tribes of Central Asia brought yet more variety and more beauties to the Tang courts. The exotic and energetic dances of the 'Western Twirling Girls' found deeply appreciative audiences in the courts of the Tang aristocracy and, of course, inspired the poets. Li He wrote:

> Wild sleeves criss-cross like bamboos
> Flute-girls were dancing . . . .[8]

Li was also captivated by the romantic quality of foreigners:

> A curly-headed nomad boy
> With eyes of green,
> By a tall mansion, in the still of the night
> Is playing his flute.[9]

There are myriad literary references to the taste for the exotic, some supported by material evidence. The Western-inspired hat and veil combination, for example, is precisely recorded on many Tang pottery tomb figurines. Such was the pace of fashion at the time that the veil was soon dropped and unveiled women were to be seen brazenly riding around the streets of Changan. An edict of 671 outlawing such conduct was issued, requiring women to ride in the traditional manner in a covered carriage, but that too was ignored. Turkish-style hats, Turkish coats and boots, leopard-skin hats and Iranian jackets were commonplace garb for the gentry of cosmopolitan Changan.

The influence of Islamic art is perfectly expressed in this glazed pottery phoenix-headed ewer of the Tang dynasty. The form is directly inspired by Sassanian Persian metal work and the principal decorative feature of the galloping horse with a hunter turning in the saddle, brandishing his bow, is a motif familiar to the Persian style.

ABOVE *The Grand Canal at Suzhou is an important commercial artery today just as it was in the Tang dynasty. The problem of communications over vast distances has always been a major challenge in China. In the Tang era effective means of communications were established, and of critical importance were the waterways, natural and man-made. Twelve centuries ago this same canal bore ships and barges carrying salt and exotic goods from India, Ceylon and the Middle East to the heart of metropolitan China in the Yellow River valley.*

RIGHT *A superb white-glazed pottery figure of a Western Asian man holding a wine flask. Here the Tang potter has captured the Chinese fascination with the foreign traders who travelled with their wares to Changan. The stylized curly hair, bulging eyes, flaring nostrils and symbolic moustache became the almost stereotyped features for the foreign image.*

The women were adorned not only with silks patterned with Sassanian-inspired decor, but also with jewellery of jade, crystal, carnelian, malachite and lapis lazuli that came from the west, ivory from the south, tortoiseshell from Annam, coral originating from Persia and Ceylon, and amber from Persia. The poet Du Fu describes them:

> The third day of the third moon, the spring air fresh,
> Changan lakeside is thronged with lovely women,
> Voluptuous in beauty, thoughts aloof, gentle and elegant,
> Gleaming skin smooth and fine, bones and flesh in symmetry,
> Dresses of silk gauze shining in the late Spring sun,
> Woven with peacocks in gold thread and unicorns in silver.
> On their heads what do they wear?
> Leaves made of Kingfish feathers garlanding their temples.
> At their backs what do we see?
> Pearl-embroidered trains, perfectly shaped to fit.[10]

The sense of the exotic was further enhanced by perfumes and incense. Sandalwood, camphor, frankincense and myrrh from the Middle East; storax from Malaya; cloves from Indonesia and cardamom from Malaya. The men's traditional Taoist search for aphrodisiacs and means to immortality brought rhinoceros horn and aromatics to the Middle Kingdom. The Emperor Xuan Zong was fed aphrodisiac pills made from 'passion flower aromatic' by his ever-eager consort Yang Guifei, to '. . . help his passion to develop into excitement and the strength of his sinews not to flag'.[11]

Although the mutton-eating habits of the Turks had been established in north China prior to the founding of the Tang dynasty, a range of more tasty and delicate foodstuffs was introduced to tempt, successfully, the courtly palate. 'Thorn honey' from Qoco, almonds from Kucha, the astringent myrobalan fruit from India, spinach from Nepal, pistachio nuts from Sodgia and Persia, olives from further west, pepper from Indochina and sesame-seed sweetcakes from Western Asia were among the titbits found at the feasts of Changan. Du Fu describes the later stages of a banquet:

> Purple steaks of camel-hump are lifted from a turquoise cauldron,
> Fresh silvery fish served in crystal dishes.
> But the chopsticks of rhinoceros-horn are plied languidly now,
> And delicate morsels are sliced by tinkling knives to no purpose.
> Mounted eunuchs gallop up, without stirring the dust,
> Sent from the Imperial kitchens with the eight
> Dainties in succession.[12]

The Middle Eastern merchants re-introduced the custom of grape-wine drinking and viniculture to China after some centuries of neglect. In the annals of Tang poetry, wine has played a perpetually inspiring role and the refreshed vogue for grape-wine in the Tang stimulated the poets as much as it did the populace. While Li Bo may have only grudgingly and suspiciously accepted some of the fashions that came from beyond the Middle Kingdom, he did not hesitate to embrace the joys of wine:

> If Heaven itself did not love wine,
> Then no wine star would shine in the sky.
> And if Earth also did not love wine,
> Earth would have no such place as Wine Fountain.
> Have I not heard that pure wine makes a sage,
> And even muddy wine can make a man wise?[13]

ABOVE *The Chinese Central Asian variant of the familiar Tang dynasty pottery tomb figure is illustrated in this model from a tomb in the region of Turfan. Such figures were seldom glazed and always painted with the bright colours typical of Buddhist temple paintings and frescoes in the region.*

7
AN ETERNAL FLOWERING
The Art of Tang Dynasty China

No other single work of art better characterizes the spirit of an age than the ubiquitous Tang horse. These pottery models of the famed Ferghana horses, which were recovered from the tombs of the Tang royal families, the aristocracy and the military, have gained fame through their beauty and majesty, and infamy through being probably the most often faked of any works of art. In their strength and presence these magnificent models embody the qualities of realism, naturalism, confidence and technical accomplishment that are the hallmarks of Tang art.

This supreme confidence, allied to the artistic and decorative vision upon which Tang art was established, was achieved through the ready acceptance and absorption of fresh cultural influences from abroad. For example, metal and glass work from the Sassanian Empire provided the inspiration in both form and decoration for much of the colourful *sancai* three-colour glazed ceramics of the Tang, and yet these ceramics are unquestionably and distinctively Chinese.

Similarly, Tang gold and silver work achieved a high point in technical and decorative excellence which is unparalleled in the history of Chinese art, but this tradition too had foreign origins. Buddhist sculpture attained a distinctive peak, due to a combination of fresh influences from India, strong imperial patronage, and the increasing popularity of the religion. The continuous flow of merchants, traders and ambassadors provided constant refreshment for the insatiable Tang artists and craftsmen.

Perhaps the most pervasive and rewarding influence on the art of Tang China was that of realism. The extraordinary range of pottery tomb figures, from horses and camels to Semitic merchants and South-East Asian dancers, echoes the colourful bustle and courtly splendour of the great metropolitan centres. Their value as historical documents apart, they are works of art in a tradition of realistic sculpture which achieved its fulfilment in the seventh and eighth centuries. In the monumental stone sculptures of Buddhist art, too, there is a concern for naturalism in concept and for realism in detail. The landscape-painting tradition, which was to become the guiding principle in Chinese painting of the Song, Yuan, Ming and Qing dynasties, also had its origins in the Tang dynasty. The great masters, Wang Wei and Wu Daozi, sought and found a new form of expression based on experience and on inspiration drawn directly from nature.

In considering the character of Tang dynasty art three broad approaches can be distinguished: the realistic, the decorative and the philosophic (or expressive). These categories span all spheres of artistic endeavour and achievement.

Detail of the landscape elements in the anonymous painting The Flight of the Emperor Ming Huang to Shu *(see page 37), showing the characteristic realism of the Tang 'blue and green' style. While the towering peaks and craggy valleys cannot represent an actual landscape, the clarity and precision of the style vividly express the new vision of Tang China.*

The concepts of realism in Tang painting were founded upon the visual and psychological realism that had developed in the preceding Northern and Southern dynasties period. The great figurative painters of that time, of whom Gu Kaizhi is the most renowned, observed and depicted people in relation to one another, in situations in which the discourse between them created mood and tension. The linear style of painting, which had developed out of Han dynasty painting and calligraphy, was the ideal mode of expression for the precise and poignant realism which reached its apogee during the Tang.

The great realist painters of the Tang dynasty confined themselves essentially to figurative subjects. However, the expression in the definitive brush line was the quality that artists such as Yan Liben (seventh century), Han Gan and Zhou Fang (eighth century) sought. It was a means of expression in total accord with Chinese linear and calligraphic qualities; one indeed that had been identified by earlier critics and writers as the spiritual essence of painting. The pervasive qualities of the mysterious *qiyun*, 'spirit resonance', were regarded as the most essential in painting and headed the list of prerequisites known as the 'six canons' of painting. These were formulated originally by the writer-critic Xie He at the end of the fifth century and outlined in his *Gu Hua Pin Lu* (*Treatise on Painting*). It was the quality of 'spirit resonance' above all others that determined the true expressive line. The great Tang art historian Zhang Yanyuan wrote (c. 845) in his *Li Dai Ming Hua Ji*, known as *The Origin of Painting*: '. . . painting must be sought for beyond the shapes . . .'.[1] Line had progressed from a means merely to determine shape and form to a means by which, through inflection, variable strength and inner expressive quality, one could define something of the character and spirit of the subject, whether a human figure, a feature of the natural world or even a man-made object. Expressive line was the determining and distinctive feature of Tang dynasty realistic painting.

These attributes place Tang realistic painting firmly within the classic Chinese tradition. However, it must be recognized that contacts with Western styles, which were more concerned with naturalistic realism than with modes of expression within their artistic traditions, exercised a considerable influence on Chinese art. This is seen particularly in aspects of Buddhist painting.

Notions of realism were also the basis for a particular and distinctive form of early landscape painting that flourished in the Tang dynasty before the genre became a vehicle for personal expression embodying philosophic values. This landscape style too had its origins in the linear style of the preceding era, but attained new heights of realism in both composition and execution in the Tang under the auspices of such artists as Li Sixun (651–c.718) and Li Zhaodao (eighth century). Indeed, it was during the Tang that the idea of the landscape as an appropriate subject in itself, rather than merely a setting for a figurative subject, was promoted and accepted. In their quest for realism if not accuracy these artists employed colour to often dramatic effect, giving birth to the so-called 'Tang blue and green' style of landscape painting. Although relatively shortlived as an emphatic and motivating style, it gave pure landscape painting a starting point and also continued to be a point of reference for painters throughout the dynastic history of China.

The glory of Tang art is characterized by magnificent pottery models of the proud Ferghana horse. The volumes and proportions echo the sense of naturalism and the detailed modelling of features, including harness and bridle fittings, is enhanced by the rich cream, amber and blue glazes. Much less usual is the blue-glazed saddlecloth on this classic and enduringly beautiful example.

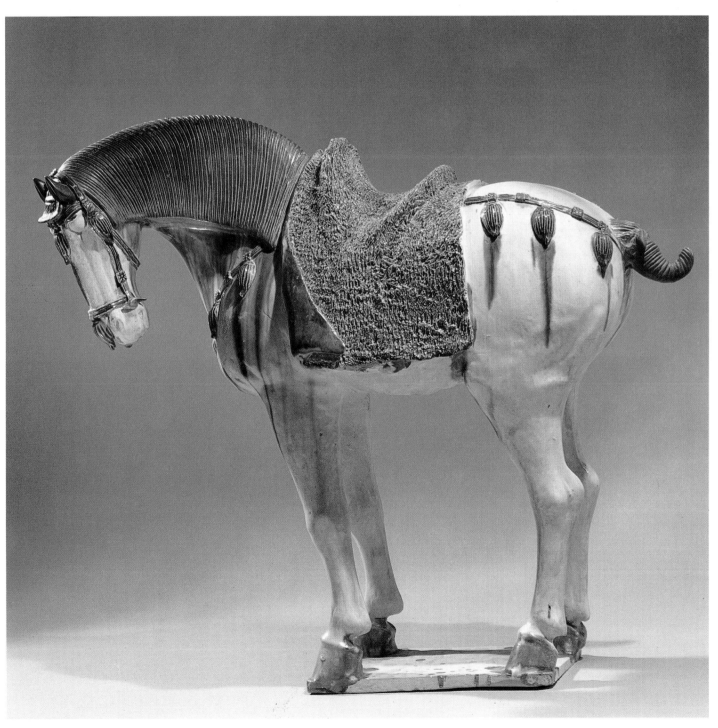

The essential characteristics of the linear, realistic landscape style also appear in a small number of isolated examples, including murals at the Dunhuang Buddhist cave temples, murals on the entrance walls to Tang imperial tombs, an extraordinary group of objects which include musical instruments in the Shōsō-in at Nara in Japan, and some fragmentary scrolls, both secular and Buddhist. This last group includes a number of later works, copies based on Tang originals to variable degrees of faithfulness.

In ceramics, realism was a prerequisite to the tomb figure tradition. The cultivated and decorous life at the courts is vividly recorded in the tomb accoutrements, representing the worldly paraphernalia of the deceased. For those facsimiles to properly fulfil their role, fidelity to appearance was essential. Painted, lead-glazed

A miniature gilt bronze Buddhist reliquary just 14cm (5.5in) high in the form of a building, dating from the late Tang dynasty, ornamented with miniature Buddhas in relief around the central image of the Bodhisattva Guanyin seated on a lotus.

A sancai *three-colour glazed pottery offering dish standing on three small feet based on a metal-work form. The stylized floral band surrounding a medallion with a bird in flight is inspired by Western Asian decorative styles but the final product is wholly Chinese and a perfect expression of the Tang aesthetic.*

or both, and sometimes even with gilded embellishments, such pottery models – ranging from the miniature to almost one-third life-size – were produced in staggering quantities in order to satisfy the demands to stack the tombs of the establishment with a prepossessing array of figures that reflected, and often surreptitiously enhanced, the status of the deceased.

The tomb figure tradition had its origins in the burial customs of late Bronze Age China, when the practice of making facsimiles was introduced, supplanting the barbarous custom of burying the actual servants of the deceased. The tradition flourished in the Han dynasty and reached its colourful apogee in the Tang. In this, probably more than in any other form, the Tang sense of realism, feeling for colour, taste for variety and delight in the exotic are given marvellous expression.

Pottery figures were made of earthenware, usually of a buff-pink colour or sometimes grey. Either they were covered with a white slip that served as a base for painted details or they were glazed with a single colour, or a combination of three colours. When models of human figures were glazed, the heads and faces were invariably left unglazed, thus permitting the detailed features to be painted. A small number of figures were both glazed and painted, generally with the paint applied over a bland straw-coloured glaze. Additional gilded highlights were rare and tended to be confined to figures of particular distinction.

The attention to detail, to decorative features, harness fittings, loads to the pack camels with items of cargo clearly defined, and patterns in the silk robes of the courtly ladies, illustrates the Tang predilection for minutiae in the quest for realism. This also extends to other media. The mural paintings on the walls of the Tang tombs depicting courtly attendants, polo players and other figurative subjects provide a direct comparison with the three-dimensional pottery models.

In the diversified arts of Buddhism, which in China reached their zenith in the Tang, the demands for realistic representation are apparent. The role of art in the service of the religion was fundamentally iconographic; nonetheless, realism in the

representation of deities, natural elements, architectural features and supporting secular figures was part of the overall iconography and helped Buddhism to gain a wider audience and more credibility. Nowhere is this more positively illustrated than in the wall paintings at the Dunhuang Buddhist cave temples in the far western Gansu province. This oasis town, which featured prominently in the history of the Silk Road, became an important place of pilgrimage for adherents of Buddhism. The cave temples, founded in the fourth century, flourished in the Tang when a large number of new caves were established and decorated with vibrant paintings, essentially Chinese in character, but in colour, broad defining outline and subject matter displaying certain Indo-Iranian influences. The distinctive Chinese expressive linear style of painting was to emerge at Dunhuang in the mid-Tang and to provide the existing concepts of realism in Buddhist art with a fresh initiative towards the visual and psychological realism characteristic of secular figure and landscape painting.

Outstanding among the Dunhuang paintings that express Tang realism in their colour, quality and definition are a number of figurative and landscape passages. The more literary themes, such as the *Jataka* themes or stories from the life of Sakyamuni Buddha, and particular details from the *sutras* or Buddhist scriptures, required a realistic rendering of the figures and the environment in order to make them credible. Distinctive figures or figure types, landscape and natural features, animals and architectural features are drawn with a linear precision.

RIGHT *A glazed pottery figure of a tomb guardian or* lokopala *in which the attention to detail serves to heighten the reality and presence of this awesome protector of the dead, here trampling a demon. Unlike in the West, the human figure has never played more than a symbolic role in the art of China and in such ceramic sculptures recognition of the true anatomy of human form was subjugated to the needs of ritual. The phoenix, symbol of the empress, that ornaments the helmet is only supposed to appear in times of peace and prosperity, and it may be assumed that its frequent appearance on the helmets of these guardian figures suggests a role as protector of peace within the tomb.*

LEFT *Glazed pottery tomb figure of a foreigner holding a wine ewer in the form of a goose. A number of such models, presumably of wine merchants, are known although the significance of the goose-form ewer is a mystery. In Chinese mythology the goose has no great significance, other than as an emblem of the married state, and its appearance in this unique form may be an allusion to foreign origins.*

A woven silk fragment made in Tang China but with a pearl-bordered roundel design encompassing a deer that was directly inspired by contemporary Sassanian Persian art. The vast majority of surviving Chinese silks of the Tang dynasty have been recovered from tombs and sites along the Silk Road, indicating that they were popular not only with the gregarious Chinese of the time but also in the markets of Western Asia and the Eastern Mediterranean.

Illustrations from the *sutras*, such as the *Lotus Sutra* in caves 23 and 103 and the popular *Pure Land Sutra* in cave 172, use the landscape to illustrate parables described in the text. Characteristic of such landscape passages is the high viewpoint adopted by the artist, which gives the viewer a grand vista and the appropriate sense of depth and recession. Ranges of hills and interlocking valleys stretch into the background in an immature form of perspective.

The art of figurative sculpture in China was principally exercised (the pottery tomb figure tradition apart) through monumental works in stone that lined the spirit roads to the great tombs and, above all, in the service of Buddhism. Buddhist sculpture was unreservedly iconographic, unlike painting which, in its commitment to literary themes, adopted a wider repertoire; but the sculpture too shows a concern for realism in the expression of form and volume. The three major cave-temple complexes of the Tang, Tianlong Shan in Shanxi province, Longmen near Loyang in Henan province and Dunhuang in Gansu province, display refreshing Indian influences. These precipitated the break with the earlier formalized analytical style of the late fifth and sixth centuries. Such developments are most persuasively realized in the figures and deities supporting the main Buddha image, such as Bodhisattvas, monks, acolytes and guardians. The Bodhisattva image in particular attained in the Tang dynasty a fluency in outline, form and relative volumes that bordered on sensuality. The guardian figures, such as the massive *dvarapalas* in the Fengxian temple at Longmen, acquired, through realism of detail and concept, a quality that is positively heroic.

Formal decorative patterns employing essentially floral designs form the largest and most varied group in Tang decorative art. Lotus scrolls, leaf scrolls, palmette and half-palmette motifs, peony scrolls and sprays were the most popular subjects formulated in repetitive designs for gold and silver bowls and cups, bronze mirror-backs, textiles and, to a more limited extent, three-colour glaze (*sancai*) ceramic vessels. All such designs became firmly identified with the Tang tradition and style, but most had their origins, in concept if not subject matter, in non-Chinese culture. Specific features, such as the lotus design and the palmette, came with Buddhism; others, such as the medallion motif, arrived with Sassanian metal work.

Formal motifs, which include 'heraldic' devices and pearl-bordered roundels, were also inspired through the import of foreign goods to China. Such designs found special favour in the repetitive patterns for woven silks and may have been further stimulated by the demands of the export trade. The confronting bird or animal motif, familiar in Sassanian designs, is frequently seen on Tang silks which, on the evidence of their having been found at sites along the silk routes, were probably destined for the markets of West Asia. These designs, having established themselves within the Chinese tradition, then found their way further east to Japan. The pearl-bordered roundel, perhaps encompassing a bird in flight or a

ABOVE *An unusual and refined example of Tang metal craftsmanship is this small melon-shaped box and cover made of parcel-gilt silver. Each of the eight lobed segments is ornamented in the repoussé technique with varying designs of birds and scrolling vines.*

RIGHT *Reverse side of a small Tang dynasty bronze mirror of lobed shape with an unusual silver-gilt repoussé design of four semi-human figures and a scrolling floral pattern around a central crouching animal. Just 6cm (2.4in) in diameter, this mirror is a consummate expression of Tang craftsmanship and the lively elegance of an artistic tradition that embraced a naturalistic vision with inherent Chinese formalism.*

Perfect harmony of form and expression in a globular pottery jar on which the coloured glazes have been controlled to run around the contours of the vessel and form a design that, while unmistakably Tang Chinese, has a conspicuously contemporary flavour.

BELOW *The sophisticated elegance and restraint of a plain white-glazed jar and cover shows the strength of tradition and formalism in the art of Tang dynasty China.*

stylized floral motif, was among those of essentially foreign inspiration which were frequently used to ornament *sancai* ceramic vessels.

Realistic motifs were also embodied in less formal decorative patterns. Such 'scattered' patterns were used on gold and silver vessels, mirror-backs, silks and ceramics. These designs, employing figurative elements, hunters, animals and birds in particular, were favoured for a range of amphora-like vessels whose shape had been determined by Sassanian metal-work ewers.

The Tang taste for showy and colourful decorative effect is particularly well illustrated in the enormous range of *sancai* glazed ceramics, the decoration of which has no base in realism but merely delights the eye in its effective use of vivid, splashed-glaze colours. The notion of such abstract and expressive decoration has no real predecessor in the formal traditions of the arts of China, and indeed has no successor. It must be seen as a peculiarly Tang phenomenon. Earthenware vessels, offering-plates, jars, ewers, amphoras, tripod jars and trays, decorated with a combination of three colours from a range of green, blue, amber, cream, yellow-ochre and occasionally black lead glazes, are an established hallmark of the Tang ceramic style. Another variation on the same theme, but one with a more controlled effect, is found on stoneware vessels with a blue-black glaze with pale blue, almost white, mottling. So characteristic of the nature and flavour of the Tang dynasty were these *sancai* and related ceramic wares that production virtually ceased upon the demise of the dynasty. They survive as evocative emblems of a golden age.

The different philosophic and expressive approaches to art are well illustrated by the iconographic formalism of Buddhist art and the less formal, more intellectual forum of painting and calligraphy.

The strength of the monumental Buddhist sculptures relies partly upon their realism but equally upon the depth of the spiritual commitment of the artists. The

tense style, formalized almost to the point of abstraction, of early sixth-century Buddhist sculpture is rightly regarded as a high point for the art in China, but the relaxing and humanizing realism of the Tang stone sculptures of the cave temples, particularly Tianlong Shan, is more appealing. The very fact that such images acquired in the Tang a more human identity lent strength to the religious conviction they expressed. Such developments in the physical appearance of the icons were determined by aesthetic and stylistic factors as well as by developments in the Buddhist faith itself. In particular, the growing popularity of the *Paradise Sutras* made real the promise of after-life in Paradise through the earth-bound Bodhisattva deity. The broad, subjective appeal of such an ideology is reflected in the easy, seductive style of the icons.

One of the most significant and enduring developments in thought and expression during the Tang dynasty was the emergence of the idea that painting and calligraphy might serve as a means of personal and philosophic expression. The artistic foundations to such expression lie in the linear realism of the classic Tang painting style. To this was added the cultivation of the mental image and the spontaneous qualities of pure brushwork, which combined to divert the artist away from realism and towards an idealized intellectual image. These developments laid the tentative foundations for the subsequent emergence of the *wenren*, or literary man's style, which championed the cause of landscape painting in the Song, Yuan, Ming and Qing dynasties.

In the fourth and fifth centuries the landscape had played a limited, almost symbolic role, providing a token natural setting for figurative subjects. The landscape was thus associated with the expression of those ideas and values that were part of the figurative story. In the Tang, the landscape itself began to emerge as a subject in its own right; this later became an ideal, to induce the appropriate mood and spiritual response to the natural world and thus assist in Tao, the communion between Man and nature. Even in the early realistic landscape paintings, such as those at the Dunhuang temples, the jagged, angular strokes suggest an expression beyond linear definition. It is as though the brushstrokes themselves sought to define the inner strength of the natural world.

This new approach to the role of painting, of landscape painting in particular, brought that art closer to the realms of philosophic debate, literature and calligraphy. In the vanguard of this influential movement were two intellectual giants of the Tang dynasty, Wang Wei and Wu Daozi. While hardly any tangible evidence of their genius as artists survives, literary records accord them both legendary powers through which they instilled true spirit into the brushline.

Wang Wei (699–759) is attributed with having initiated the *pomo*, or 'broken ink', style of monochrome ink painting. It was a style in which accented strokes broke the evenness of a brushline or a wash and additional strokes created a surface texture. Such devices for the expression of feeling became fundamental to the later *wenren*, literary man's tradition. The great scholar-gentleman painter of the late Ming dynasty, Dong Qichang, who considered Wang Wei the originator of the only means of true expression, wrote in a colophon to one of his own paintings:

> The painters before Wang Wei were not lacking in skill, only they could not transmit the spiritual quality of a landscape; they were still separated from this by worldly thoughts . . . . Wang Wei's landscapes are of the divine class.[2]

In his time Wang Wei was noted as much for his poetry as for his painting although he wrote of himself:

> In this present world
> I am wrongly called a poet;
> In a former existence
> I must have been a painter.[3]

His poetry, too, was principally devoted to exploring the beauty of nature and to expressing the enduring and regenerative powers of nature and the universe. As in his painting, so in his poetry Wang sought to express the moving spirit rather than the physical appearance. He was one of the very first of the great tradition of poet-scholar painters. He was the forerunner of what is perhaps the most significant and pervasive style of Chinese painting, the literati-style landscape.

Although recognized as the leading figurative painter of his day, Wu Daozi, an older contemporary of Wang Wei, also painted landscapes which, though done in wholly expressive brushwork, had a spiritual quality transcending reality. According to the ninth-century critic Zhang Yanyuan, Wu was the only painter who achieved complete mastery of Xie He's 'Six Principles'. Of Wu, the critic wrote: 'He exhausted completely the creative power of nature and the resonance of the spirit was so overwhelmingly strong that it could hardly be confined to the silk.'[4]

The spontaneity of Wu Daozi's painting was the source of its strength. One of his greatest admirers, the Emperor Xuan Zong, is reputed to have said: 'Li Sixun's achievement of many months, and Wu Daozi's of a single day, both reach the

From the Tang era to the present day, certain spectacular mountainscapes and towering pinnacles of rock have inspired the poets and painters of China. One of these is Huangshan in Anhui province, where soaring peaks and wonderfully intimate moments that truly seem to bring mankind close to the spirit of nature and the powers of the universe. It is here that the art of Chinese painting becomes a reality.

extreme of excellence.'[5] It was the 'untramelled energy' of his brush that gave each line a strength and purpose beyond definition. But his freedom in the use of brush and ink was not confined to pure line, for he is credited with having introduced the use of graded washes and tones to evoke depth and atmosphere. Wu's ability to express the underlying spirit of his subject, whether a landscape, a human figure, a bird or an animal, gave rise to some extravagant observations on his genius. The mid-ninth-century critic Zhu Jingxuan notes: 'He also painted five dragons in the Inner Hall whose scales and horny parts seem to be in swift motion. When it is about to rain, a mist comes from them.'[6]

Perhaps the final comment on Wu Daozi can also be used as a comment on the Tang dynasty, that period of noble and gregarious self-confidence that has ever since been viewed as an eternal source of inspiration for a great and continuing civilization: 'Everything that he ever painted has been used as a model by men of later generations.'[7]

ABOVE *The carved sandstone head of a Bodhisattva, one who had attained enlightenment but remained earth-bound in order to bring salvation to all, from the Tianlong Shan cave temples. Although aloof, the face has a true sense of realism in the detail and an almost female countenance in the round, fleshy face and pouting mouth. The nature of the sandstone of the Tianlong Shan terrain permitted delicate detail carving and the achievement of a soft overall texture well suited to the more plastic style of sculpture then current, as illustrated in this head.*

RIGHT *Detail of* The Flight of the Emperor Ming Huang to Shu *(see page 37), which records the flight of the Emperor Xuan Zong (or Ming Huang) and his concubine, the beautiful Yang Guifei, from the An Lushan rebellion. The section of the imperial entourage shown here is depicted in superb detail, typical of the realism and expressiveness of Tang art.*

The Tang dynasty has left an unmistakable and indelible mark on the style and character of the Middle Kingdom. Seen by the Chinese of today as a remote and distant pinnacle in their history, it is always remembered as a golden age, an age of achievement and artistic enrichment and a perpetual source of inspiration. It is impossible to escape the impact of the Tang dynasty as almost daily archaeological discoveries open new horizons of achievement. Such finds continue to fuel the contemporary imagination as notions and tokens of the era appear – in fashion, theatre, music, architecture, calligraphy and of course in paintings such as this, where that most evocative and romantic emblem of the dynasty, the Silk Road, remains a favoured theme.

NOTES

CHAPTER 1

1 Quoted in Woodbridge Bingham *The Founding of the T'ang Dynasty* Baltimore, 1941, p.51.
2 *Tang shu* (Book of the Tang), chap. 5. Quoted in Bingham *op. cit.* p.108.
3 Quoted in A.F. Wright and D. Twitchett (ed.) *Perspectives on the T'ang* New Haven and London, 1973, p.51.

CHAPTER 2

1 Quoted in Wm. Theodore de Bary (ed.) *Sources of Chinese Tradition* Vol. 1, Columbia University Press, 1964, p.158.
2 Confucius, *Analects* Book II Wei Jing, Chaps. I–III.
3 *Mencius* Book VII, part 2, chap. 14. See James R. Ware, *The Sayings of Mencius* Taipei, 1980. Quoted in part in de Bary *op. cit.* p.96.
4 *Hsün Tzu (Xun Zi) Basic Writings*; translated by Burton Watson, Columbia University Press, 1963, p.37.
5 H.A. Giles *A Chinese Biographical Dictionary* entry 2264 on Wei Cheng.
6 Quoted in Howard J. Weschler *Mirror to the Son of Heaven* (Wei Cheng at the Court of T'ang T'ai-tsung), Yale University Press, 1974, p.143.
7 Aisin-Gioro Pu Yi *From Emperor to Citizen* Peking, 1979, Vol. 1, pp.58–9. Also quoted in R. Dawson *The Chinese Experience* London, 1978, p.21.
8 Quoted in D. Twitchett and J.K. Fairbank (ed.) *The Cambridge History of China* Vol. 3 Sui and T'ang China pt. 1, Cambridge University Press, 1979, p.257.
9 Aisin-Gioro Pu Yi *op. cit.* p.62.

CHAPTER 3

1 *Li Ji* ch. 10. Quoted in Fung Yu-lan *A Short History of Chinese Philosophy* New York, 1948, p.155.
2 Confucius *Analects* Book XVII Yang He, chap. 2. Quoted in variant form in de Bary *op. cit.* p.23.
3 Confucius *Analects* Book IV Li Ren, chap. 2. Quoted in variant form in de Bary *op. cit.* p.26.
4 de Bary *op. cit.* p.45.
5 de Bary *op. cit.* p.45.
6 *Mencius* Book II pt. 1, chap. 3. Quoted in de Bary *op. cit.* p.93.
7 *Hsün Tzu Basic Writings*, Watson *op. cit.* sec. 23.
8 *Hsün Tzu Basic Writings*, Watson *op. cit.* sec. 21. See also Dawson *op. cit.* p.38.
9 Wright and Twitchett *op. cit.* p.322.
10 Zhuang Zi *Zhuang Zi* chap. 8. Quoted in Fung Yu-lan *op. cit.* pp.105–6.
11 Lao Zi *Dao De Jing* 18 and 19. Quoted in Dawson *op. cit.* p.99 and de Bary *op. cit.* p.55.
12 *Zhuang Zi* chap. 3. Quoted in Dawson *op. cit.* p.98.
13 *Shi Ji* (Records of the Historian), chap. 63. Quoted in Dawson *op. cit.* pp.99–100.
14 Giles *op. cit.* entry 978.
15 *Baopu Zi* chap. 2. Quoted in de Bary *op. cit.* p.259.
16 *Baopu Zi* chap. 4. Quoted in de Bary *op. cit.* p.261.
17 *Baopu Zi* chap. 3. Quoted in de Bary *op. cit.* p.262.
18 *Baopu Zi* chap. 6. Quoted in de Bary *op. cit.* p.262.
19 See K. Ch'en *Buddhism in China* Princeton University, 1964, p.69.

CHAPTER 4

1 de Bary *op. cit.* p.376.
2 Ch'en *op. cit.* p.355.
3 Ch'en *op. cit.* p.355.
4 de Bary *op. cit.* pp.372–3.
5 C. Birch (ed.) *Anthology of Chinese Literature* New York, 1965, pp.253–4.
6 de Bary *op. cit.* p.371.
7 Wright and Twitchett *op. cit.* p.360.
8 'Self Abandonment' by Li Bo. Translated in A. Waley *Chinese Poems* London, 1961, p.103.
9 'On Hearing Chün, a Monk from Shu, Play the Lute' by Li Bo. In Innes Herdan *300 T'ang Poems* Taipei, 1973, p.232.
10 'To the Assistant Prefect Chang' by Wang Wei. Birch *op. cit.* p.224.
11 Ch'en *op. cit.* p.236.

CHAPTER 5

1 M. Broomhall *Islam in China*, London, 1910, pp.45.6. See also Jane Gaston Mahler *The Westerners Among the Figurines of the T'ang Dynasty of China* Rome, 1959, p.103.
2 'To His Old Friend Xin' by Li Bo. In Birch *op. cit.* p.228.
3. 'Climbing the Terrace of Guanyin and Looking at the City of Changan' by Bo Zhuyi. In Waley *op. cit.* p.161.
4. Edward H. Schafer *The Golden Peaches of Samarkand* University of California, 1963, p.27.
5. Paul Wheatley *The Pivot of the Four Quarters* University of Edinburgh, 1971, p.175. See also Dawson *op. cit.* pp.13–14.
6. Dawson *op. cit.* p.14.
7 The Ming Tang is also described in C.P. Fitzgerald *The Empress Wu* University of British Columbia, 1968, pp.131–3.

CHAPTER 6

1 *Along The Ancient Silk Routes. Central Asian Art from the West Berlin State Museums.* Exhibition catalogue, Metropolitan Museum of Art, New York, 1982, p.28.
2 Xuan Zang *Records of the Western Regions*. Quoted in S. Beal (trans.) *The Life of Hiuen-Tsiang* (Xuan Zang), London, 1911, pp.21–2.
3 Schafer *op. cit.* p.14.
4 Schafer *op. cit.* p.8.
5 'On Leaving the City and parting from Zhang Yuxin' by Li He. Translated by J.D. Frodsham *The Poems of Li Ho* (Li He), Oxford, 1970, p.250.
6 Schafer *op. cit.* p.21 from a poem by Li Bo.
7 A description by the Buddhist priest Jian Zhen who visited Canton in AD 748. See Schafer *op. cit.* p.15.
8 'Joys of the Rich' by Li He. Frodsham *op. cit.* p.202.
9 'Song: Dragons at Midnight' by Li He. Frodsham *op. cit.* p.274.
10 'A Ballad of Lovely Women' by Du Fu. Herdan *op. cit.* p.212.
11 Schafer *op. cit.* p.158.
12 'A Ballad of Lovely Women' by Du Fu. Herdan *op. cit.* p.212.
13 'Four Poems on Wine' by Li Bo. Birch *op. cit.* p.230.

CHAPTER 7

1 O. Siren *The Chinese on the Art of Painting* New York, 1963, p.28.
2 L. Calvin and D.B. Walmsley *Wang Wei the Painter-Poet* Rutland and Toyko, 1968, pp.144–5.
3 William Acker *Some T'ang and Pre-T'ang Texts on Chinese Painting* Leiden, 1974, p.265.
4 Siren *op. cit.* p.23.
5 Acker *op. cit.* p.235.
6 Acker *op. cit.* p.235.
7 Acker *op. cit.* p.236.

BIBLIOGRAPHY

Acker, William, P.B., *Some T'ang and Pre-T'ang Texts on Chinese Painting*, 2 vols. E.J. Brill, Leiden, 1974

Akiyama, T., et al. *Arts of China: Neolithic Cultures to the T'ang Dynasty. Recent Discoveries*, Kodansha International, Tokyo and Palo Alto, 1968

Akiyama, T., et al. *Art of China: Buddhist Cave Temples. New Researches*, Kodansha International, Tokyo and Palo Alto, 1969

de Bary, Wm Theodre, Chan, Wing-tsit and Watson, Burton, *Sources of Chinese Tradition*, Columbia University Press, New York and London, 1960

Bingham, Woodbridge, *The Founding of the T'ang Dynasty. The Fall of Sui and Rise of T'ang*, Waverly Press, Baltimore, 1941

Birch, Cyril (ed.), *Anthology of Chinese Literature*, Grove Press, New York, 1965

Broomhall, Marshall, *Islam in China. A Neglected Problem*, London, 1910

Ch'en, Kenneth K.S., *Buddhism in China*, Princeton University Press, Princeton, New Jersey, 1964

Cooper, Arthur (selected and trans.), *Li Po and Tu Fu*, Penguin, Harmondsworth, 1973, 1974, 1976

David, Sir Percival, *Chinese Connoisseurship. The Ko Ku Yao Lun*, Faber and Faber, London, 1971

Dawson, Raymond, *Imperial China*, Hutchinson, London, 1972

Dawson, Raymond, *The Chinese Experience*, Weidenfeld and Nicholson, London, 1978

Dunhuang, Institute for Cultural Relics, *The Art Treasures of Dunhuang*, Joint Publishing Co., Hong Kong and Lee Publishers Group, New York, 1981

Fitzgerald, C.P., *Son of Heaven. A Biography of Li Shih-min, founder of the T'ang Dynasty*, Cambridge University Press, Cambridge, 1933

Fitzgerald, C.P., *China: A Short Cultural History*, 1st ed. 1935, 2nd ed. 1950, 3rd ed. Cresset Press, London, 1961

Fitzgerald, C.P., *The Empress Wu*, University of British Columbia Press, Vancouver, 1968

Frodsham, J.D. (trans.), *The Poems of Li Ho 791–817*, Clarendon Press, Oxford, 1970

Fung, Yu-lan, *A Short History of Chinese Philosophy*, Macmillan, London, 1948; 2nd ed. 1966; 3rd ed. London and New York, 1968

Herdan, Innes (trans.), *300 T'ang Poems*, Far East Book Co., Taipei, 1973

Hucker, Charles O., *China's Imperial Past*, Duckworth, London, 1975

Loehr, Max, *The Great Painters of China*, Phaidon Press, Oxford, 1980

Longmen, Cultural Properties Bureau, *Longmen Shiku* (The Longmen Cave Temples). Cultural Relics Publishing House, Beijing, 1980

Los Angeles, County Museum, *The Arts of the T'ang Dynasty* (exhibition catalogue). Los Angeles, 1957

Mahler, Jane Gaston, *The Westerners Among the Figurines of the T'ang Dynasty of China*, Instituto Italiano Per il Medio ed Estremo Oriente, Rome, 1959

Medley, Margaret, *T'ang Pottery and Porcelain*, Faber and Faber, London, 1981

New York, Metropolitan Museum of Art, *Along the Ancient Silk Routes. Central Asian Art from the West Berlin State Museums* (exhibition catalogue). New York, 1982

Reischauer, Edwin O., *Ennin's Travels in T'ang China*, Ronald Press, New York, 1955

Reischauer, Edwin O. and Fairbank, John K., *East Asia: the Great Tradition*, Houghton Mifflin, Boston, 1958 and 1960

Ronan, Colin A., *The Shorter Science and Civilization in China: 1* (an abridgement of Joseph Needham's original text). Cambridge University Press, Cambridge, 1978 and 1980

Rowland, Benjamin, *The Evolution of the Buddha Image* (exhibition catalogue). Asia Society, New York, 1963

Schafer, Edward H., *The Golden Peaches of Samarkand. A Study of T'ang Exotics*, University of California Press, Berkeley and Los Angeles, 1963

Schafer, Edward H., *The Vermilion Bird. T'ang Images of the South*, University of California Press, Berkeley and Los Angeles, 1967

Schafer, Edward H., *The Divine Woman. Dragon Ladies and Rain Maidens in T'ang Literature*, University of California Press, Berkeley, Los Angeles and London, 1973

Schloss, Ezekiel, *Ancient Chinese Ceramic Sculpture: from Han through T'ang*, 2 vols. Castle Publishing, Stamford, Conn., 1977

Sickman, Laurence and Soper, Alexander, *The Art and Architecture of China*, 3rd ed. Penguin, Harmondsworth, 1968

Siren, Osvald, *The Chinese on the Art of Painting*, Schoken Books, New York and Hong Kong University Press, Hong Kong, 1963

Stein, Sir Aurel, *On Central-Asian Tracks*, University of Chicago Press, Chicago and London, 1964

Sullivan, Michael, *Chinese Landscape Painting of the Sui and T'ang Dynasties*, University of California Press, Berkeley, Los Angeles and London, 1980

Toronto, Royal Ontario Museum, *Silk Road: China Ships* (exhibition catalogue). Toronto, 1983

Twitchett, Denis and Fairbank, John K., *The Cambridge History of China: Vol. 3 Sui and T'ang China*, pt 1. University of Cambridge Press, Cambridge, 1979

Watson, William (ed.), *Pottery and Metalwork in T'ang China*, University of London, School of Oriental and African Studies, London, 1970

Watson, William, *Style in the Arts of China*, Penguin, Harmondsworth, 1974

Weschler, Howard J., *Mirror to the Son of Heaven. Wei Cheng at the Court of T'ai-tsung*, Yale University Press, New Haven and London, 1974

Wheatley, P., *The Pivot of the Four Quarters*, University Press, Edinburgh, 1971

Willetts, William, *Foundations of Chinese Art*, Thames and Hudson, London, 1965

Wright, Arthur F. (ed.), *Studies in Chinese Thought*, University of Chicago Press, Chicago and London, 1953

Wright, Arthur F. (ed.), *The Confucian Persuasion*, Stanford University Press, Stanford, 1960

Wright, Arthur F. and Twitchett, Denis (ed.), *Perspectives on the T'ang*, Yale University Press, New Haven and London, 1973

Xinjiang, Uighur Autonomous Region Museum, *Cultural Relics Unearthed in Xinjiang*, Cultural Relics Publishing House, Beijing, 1975

Zürcher, E., *The Buddhist Conquest of China*, 2 vols. E.J. Brill, Leiden, 1972

INDEX

Page numbers *in italic* refer to illustrations

ACKNOWLEDGEMENTS

Werner Forman and the publishers would like to acknowledge the help of the following in permitting the photography shown on the pages listed:

Art Gallery of New South Wales, Sydney: 11. British Library, London: 61 *top*. British Museum, London: 1, 26. China House of Arts, New York: 9 *top*. Christie's, New York: 84 *right*, 102. C. K. Chan, Hong Kong: 112 *bottom*. Commercial Press, Hong Kong: 114. Dallas Museum of Art: 9 *bottom*. Christian Deydier, London: 15, 74, 96 *left*. Eskenazi Ltd, London: 18, 29, 57, 80 *top*, 98 *right*, 104, 108 *right*, 113, 115 *right*. Myron Falk, New York: 10, 61 *centre*. Gerald Godfrey, Hong Kong: 34, 78, 99. Idemitsu Museum of Arts, Tokyo: 7, 84 *left*, 85, 95, 100 *right*, 103 *bottom*, 105, 109, 111, 116 *left*, 116 *right*. Brian McElney, Hong Kong: 22. Earl Morse, New York: 46. Museum of History, Taipei: 96 *right*. National Palace Museum, Taipei: 31 *bottom*, 37, 60, 69, 82 *top*, 86, 106, 108 *left*, 120 *bottom*. Private collection, Sydney: 45. Rene Rivkin, Sydney: 13. Shaanxi Provincial Museum, Xian: 40, 42, 82 *bottom*. Sotheby's, London: 14, 17, 94, 115 *left*. Victoria & Albert Museum, London: 27, 80 *bottom*. Michael B. Weisbrod Inc., New York: 83 *left*. Yamato Bunkakan, Nara: 38, 110.

Werner Forman would also like to thank the following for their help:

C. K. Chan, New York; Heidi L. F. Chang, Taipei; Christian Deydier, London; Giuseppe Eskenazi, London; T. Eto, Tokyo; Isobel Fanden, London; Chou Feng-Sen, Taipei; Gerald Godfrey, Hong Kong; Helen Han, Taipei; Lien-Lien Her, Taipei; Pang Lek Jong, Taipei; Rose Kerr, London; Chen Kuei-Miao, Taipei; Tin Hwei Lin, Taipei; Jessica Rawson, London; Mr Shirono, Gakuen Minami, Nara; Lin Shwu-Shin, Taipei; Michael Weisbrod, New York; Frances Wood, London; Pu Yuehue, Changsha; Xin Zue, Changsha.